100

THINGS TO DO IN

MIAMI

BEFORE YOU

DIE

2nd Edition

D1302108

BEACH WARNING FLAGS

Banderas de Advertencia de la Playa

- **Water Closed to Public**
- **High Hazard**
  High Surf and/or Strong Currents
- **Medium Hazard**
  Moderate Surf and/or Currents
- **Low Hazard**
  Calm Conditions, Exercise Caution
- **Dangerous Marine Life**

100

2nd Edition

THINGS TO DO IN

MIAMI

BEFORE YOU

DIE

• •

ROXANNE VARGAS &
MARUCHI MENDEZ

Library of Congress Control Number: 2018947843

ISBN: 9781681061894

Design by Jill Halpin

Printed in the United States of America
18 19 20 21 22   5 4 3 2 1

Please note that websites, phone numbers, addresses, and company names are subject to change or cancellation. We did our best to relay the most accurate information available, but due to circumstances beyond our control, please do not hold us liable for misinformation. When exploring new destinations, please do your homework before you go.

CONTENTS

• •

Outdoor and Recreation

● ●

Culture and History

● ●

Photo courtesy of Fontainebleau Miami Beach.

ACKNOWLEDGMENTS

Seeing the city you love through the eyes of a tourist is like discovering new horizons, but taking this journey with someone like Roxanne Vargas by your side is an exhilarating ride. Radiant Roxy, as I call her, redefines the meaning of "plenty." Her abundance of joy, love, generosity, and kindness combined with infinite energy make her the most plentiful person I know. I am blessed to have cowritten two books with her and hope to continue our adventures together. Thanks for working so hard, Rox. Love you to the moon and back. I also want to thank my twin granddaughters, Angie and Patty, for all their assistance, time, input, and support during these hectic months. Always remember: "I am joyful, vibrant, full of energy, and nothing can stop me." Everything is possible, and you CAN do it all!

—Maruchi

As we poured ourselves into every detail, experience, and hidden secret shared in our bucket list of how to take in the best of Miami, you, Maruchi, have helped me cross an item off my very own bucket list by bringing me along with you for this wild ride! Thank you for being my partner, my confidant, and most importantly, my friend, whom I call family. To my boys, Julian and Sebastian, I can't wait to continue checking off items on this bucket list with you and with Danny, my forever partner in life and adventure. I love you all with everything I am!

—Roxy

• •

PREFACE

Welcome to our slice of paradise, welcome to Miami!

Taste the diversity of our culture through award winning cuisine, see the art that paints the walls of our community, dance to the drum and beats of a Miami night and savor the moment of sinking your toes in the warms sand. This is Miami. This is your experience. Let us guide you along the way!

Why us? We love our home, Miami. This is where we live, love, work and play with our family and friends. Roxanne Vargas has had the privilege of being a voice for this community for fifteen years on NBC 6. Her most important titles though, are that of being a wife, a mom and a Miamian. Maruchi Mendez, an Author/divorcee/Mommy/Grandma, has lived in Miami for over fifty years. We go together like the sands of South Beach and the Atlantic Ocean, like Cuban Black Beans and white rice, like rum in a Mojito—we're a perfect match!

One question we get asked a lot is, "how did you figure out this list?!" It was hard, because we could write a bucket list with double the items to do in Miami! We have experienced these places together and with our kids, with our partners and on our own. We live, breathe and believe in Miami and how special she is. She pulses through us, and is a part of who we are.

So, as the title of our adventurous book suggests, life is short, and in a time where we are so connected, let's disconnect for a bit—and look up. Take in the views of the ocean from South Pointe Park or out at the Bay while having a meal at La Mar. Take a bite into your first stone crab or take your first Salsa lessons! Feel inspired by the evolving art community that paints our town—literally—and Miami's ever-changing skyline! It's not about

• •

tackling this bucket list because of a ticking clock, it's about the thirst for adventure and beauty, an experience Miami so perfectly and beautifully serves up for you.

Whether this is your first visit or fiftieth, even if you call Miami home, come be a tourist in our town—that's what we did to write this for you! Explore and experience the energy that pulses through every artery of this tropical oasis—from the oceans that paint our coast to the rich Latin culture that influences so much of Miami—we are unique. Come smell and see, taste and tackle our suggestions of *100 Things To Do In Miami Before You Die* we humbly and proudly offer you and your loved ones to experience here, in our home, Miami.

Roxy & Maru

FOOD AND DRINK

GET CRACKIN'
AT JOE'S STONE CRAB

Dress your best, greet the maitre'd, and take a seat inside one of the most famous restaurants in the country. Welcome to Joe's Stone Crab! Before Miami Beach was even a city, there was Joe's stone crabs. The Weiss family opened this small lunch counter in 1913, with an immense dream, a big love of food, and a killer fried fish sandwich! Today, the tuxedo-clad waiters await you for a superb dining experience, which still feels like a family dining room. James Bond claimed it to be "the best meal he had ever had" in the film *Goldfinger*, and every celebrity, food aficionado, or local celebrating a special occasion (or a "just because" occasion) comes to Joe's for a dining experience that is sure to be superb and unforgettable!

So let's get crackin' about the obvious here—the stone crabs! Claiming its roots and history, Joe's is the largest consumer of local stone crabs in South Florida. Sure, you can eat stone crabs at other places, but there's something about this place, about the way they're cracked, and the signature bib that's delicately tied around you that's just . . . mouthwatering. You must add this to your bucket list. If not for the stone crabs, then for the fried chicken. Yes, chicken! Wow, it's just divine, so at least order for the table to share!

11 Washington Ave., Miami Beach
305-673-0365
joesstonecrab.com

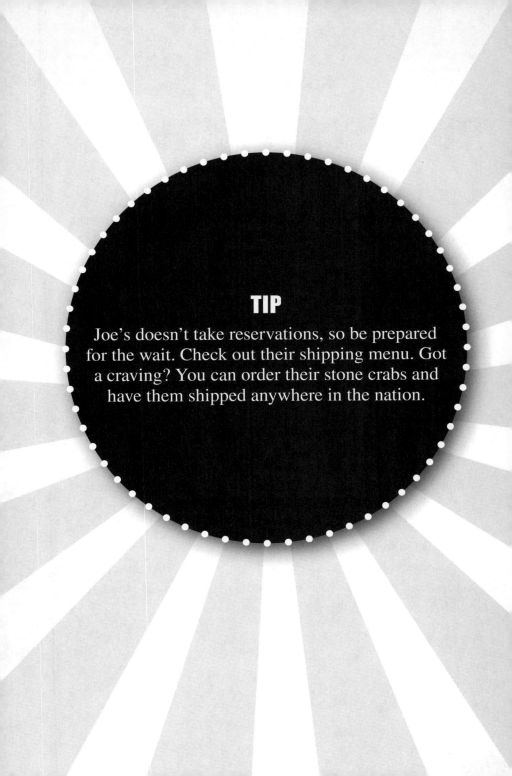

TIP

Joe's doesn't take reservations, so be prepared for the wait. Check out their shipping menu. Got a craving? You can order their stone crabs and have them shipped anywhere in the nation.

TRY THE CATCH OF THE DAY
AT BAZAAR MAR

James Beard Award-winning chef José Andrés was also world-renowned chef Ferran Adria's (Barcelona's El Bulli) student, and he thinks food is downright seductive. This is what he told Anderson Cooper in a segment of *60 Minutes*. This restaurant has been referred to as an "upscale seafood shrine." Maybe that's why you will find a giant sculpture of a fish's head with thorns in the dining room. Among the favorites is chef André's tuna crispy rice called Neptune's Pillow. It's air bread stuffed with original fresh spicy tuna and topped with tuna sashimi, soy lemon zest, and wasabi. He reinvents regular ingredients and flavors and takes them to a new dimension. One example: the marinated liquid olives, which will jolt you with elation.

Nothing compares with the drama of the Lion Fish platter—a whole breaded and fried lionfish with its fanlike fins in full display and the spectacle of the steaming clouds that rise from cryogenic carts wheeled by waiters who concoct liquid nitrogen caipirinha cocktails tableside.

Splurge in every sense and don't miss this spectacular experience because you will probably spend at least one hundred dollars per person.

1300 S Miami Ave., Miami
305-615-5859

TIP

Don't miss the Merienda Hour at
Bar Centro. Snack and sip 5:00 p.m.–7:00 p.m.

ENJOY
LE SIRENUSE RESTAURANT AND CHAMPAGNE BAR

The revival of Miami's iconic Surf Club is now a reality. The club housed Miami's most talked about lavish galas since opening in 1930 and became the gathering place of exceptional and famous people, such as Winston Churchill, Frank Sinatra, and Elizabeth Taylor. Today, two iconic cultures have come together at this historic location: The Champagne Bar and The Sirenuse of Italy's Amalfi Coast, and the luxuriousness of Miami Beach's Surf Club. Enter the exotic Mediterranean interior of mahogany, whites, and greens that have a flare of Key West, with magnolia trees adding a romantic touch. Visit the champagne bar with the best and most extensive champagne menu in town and take it all in while you enjoy the ample views of the ocean. The food is magnificent! Start off with their homemade bread, and build your appetite with their warm Caprese Calda. The lamb chops and pastas with clams or Genovese beef sauce are among the best anywhere. Tastings and treats throughout your meal are meant to pamper you and delight your palate.

9109 Collins Ave., Surfside
786-482-2280

TIP

Look out for The Surf Club Restaurant by Chef Thomas Keller. This world-renowned chef will be serving his famous food in the same hotel.

VISIT
THE FORGE

As you drive along the Arthur Godfrey Causeway or 41st Street in Miami Beach, one building's facade stands out. It should. That is the Forge, a legendary restaurant and rendezvous spot, which despite its modern renovation still exudes elegance, evokes its rich history, and remains an iconic destination. A visit to the Forge is an experience, with entertainment, music, and fun at this high-end dining destination. Start your experience at the bar with a cocktail and bar bites, where you will feel fulfilled just doing that, especially during happy hour, but we don't want you to miss out on the dining experience here! It has been nominated for the James Beard Outstanding Wine Program. Celebrities, visitors, and locals alike have all come for decades to savor the outstanding cuisine and top-notch service. Regardless of what you order for dinner, you must leave room for dessert. Have one of their famous soufflés. You're welcome!

432 W. 41st St., Miami Beach
305-538-8533

EXPERIENCE ZUMA
AT THE EPIC HOTEL

Dubbed the over-the-top "edible art" restaurant in Miami, Zuma serves Japanese dishes that will stay with you long after the visit. If you want to splurge and pay around one hundred dollars per person for the most exotic and best brunch in town, this is the place to go. Three separate buffets are offered. Whether you crave eggs or baby back ribs doused in chili, ginger, and scallions, you are in for a treat.

Taste their incredible sushi and enjoy their Asian-inspired robatayaki (robata) grill, all while delighting in breathtaking views of the terrace. Sophisticated to the ultimate degree, Zuma brings you a fun and vibrant setting that is true Miami. Be sure to try their lychee martinis.

270 Biscayne Blvd., Miami
305-577-0277

ENJOY AN OVER-THE-TOP MEAL
AT BARTON G.

Dine with a theatrical flair! Barton G. has been open in Miami Beach for almost twenty years, and it's truly a dining extravaganza with its wild presentations and tasteful sophisticated food. The minute you enter this posh ambience with its stylish and modern décor, you realize that you are seeing food through the eyes of art. Oysters in champagne and caviar that look like an octopus and salads served in a terrarium. Barton G. Weiss is known as a food designer, and at his restaurant, every dish is a topic of discussion.

Leave room for lavish desserts. Among the favorites are "popcorn surprise," with chocolate bon bons inside popcorn balls. Expect anything to decorate your plate and enjoy the fun!

P.S. Try their nitrogen cocktails.

1427 West Ave., Miami Beach
305-672-8881

EXPERIENCE MIAMI
AT KOMODO

If you are looking for an excellent dining/nightlife experience, you will find it at Komodo. Savor the Southeast Asian fare served among glass and neon in this three-story spectacular restaurant. A luxurious and posh ambience comes together for an unforgettable night, complemented by good service and swanky vibes.

The food is delicious, with the best Korean cuisine in Miami. Among the favorites are the Peking duck, tuna and toro roll, and lobster dynamite. The multilevel three-hundred-seat venue houses three bars. The third floor features the Komodo Lounge, where you can dance the night away, which makes for an ideal date night.

801 Brickell Ave., Miami
305-534-2211

TIP
Try their Caterpillar specialty roll.

SAMPLE BRUNCH FIT FOR A QUEEN
AT THE PALACE

Sit, sip, and see—and there is much to see at the world-famous Palace Bar! What makes this spot so famous? Other than being on the historic Ocean Drive strip with a stunning view of Lummus Park, all are welcome at this safe space for fun and freedom of self and expression. The food is delicious, the cocktails are mixed well, and the shows will stop traffic. No really, they'll actually stop traffic on Ocean Drive! The fiercest entertainment stars of Miami shine in the sunlight and moonlight—drag queens, such as Tiffany T. Fantasia, TP Lords, and more famous entertainers will deliver the funniest and wittiest one liners and put on a performance that'll have you immediately posting to social media to share!

1052 Ocean Dr., Miami Beach
305-5317234
palacesouthbeach.com
@PalaceSobe

SAVOR
A TRUE TASTE OF ITALY

A true South Beach gem, Casa Tua is located in Casa Tua boutique hotel. This Northern Italy Mediterranean villa houses five uniquely designed villas for those who relish the lush and intimate life. Probably one of the most quaint and romantic spots in Miami Beach, it's known for its garden, beauty, and fine authentic Italian cuisine. Among their exquisite creations are the truffle risotto, venison with sautéed spinach, and foie gras seared with tomato and natural ginger. This culinary experience might be a bit pricey, but it is worth every penny. Their service is impeccable, and you will feel like royalty.

1700 James Ave., Miami Beach
305-673-1010

TIP
Take a taste of Casa Tua Cucina, located inside Brickell City Centre, from the same Italian team that brings you this divine Italian experience!

INDULGE IN GIANNI'S
AT THE VILLA CASA CASUARINA

Step inside one of the most famous addresses in the world. It is simply known as the Versace Mansion, but this sacred space is anything but sacred. Gianni Versace fell in love with the architecture of the mansion and purchased it in 1992. Every corner, every space of The Villa oozes elegance, opulence, and artistry. Just like the late designer's style—fierce and forward, bold and unapologetic—from the facade to the intricate details inside, this iconic landmark transformed Miami Beach. The Villa is the third most photographed house in the world after the White House and Graceland.

Book an extravagant stay now at this ten-suite boutique hotel or just make a dinner reservation for the ultimate over-the-top dining experience at Gianni's. The menu reflects some of Versace's taste—a blend of Mediterranean and Italian foods influenced by Miami. You can dine in what was Versace's personal dining room, where thousands of stones were artfully placed by hand into the walls, sit on the terrace overlooking the mystical pool, or dine below in the garden right by the pool. The mosaic pool is lined with millions of tiles, thousands of which are 24-k gold. Take in all the details and look for the designer's famed design emblem, the Medusa head.

1001 Ocean Dr., Miami Beach
305-763-8026
vmmiamibeach.com

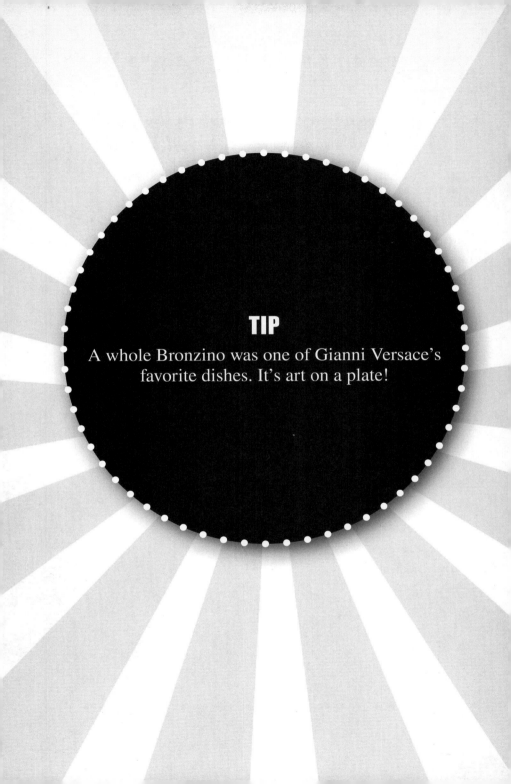

TIP

A whole Bronzino was one of Gianni Versace's favorite dishes. It's art on a plate!

JOURNEY TO EL CIELO,
AN EXCLUSIVE EXPERIENCE

Set aside three to four hours to dine at this fifty-six-seat exciting journey of molecular gastronomy. With a modern Colombian flare, this waterfront eatery has it all—the view, amber lighting, and a stunning décor. At age twenty-nine, owner and chef Juan Manuel Barrientos's restaurant in Medellin, Colombia, was named among the top 50 in Latin America. The experience begins with a sensory treat of a rose spa to cleanse your hands. So get ready and prepare for the journey. With only one seating per night, sit back in the leather chairs and enjoy either the sixteen-course epicurean menu or wine pairing, or you can choose from their unique menu a la carte. It's a true epicurean experience that incorporates the new molecular gastronomy and art into its fine cuisine.

31 SE 5th St., Miami
305-755-8840

EXPERIENCE CAFÉ ROVAL,
A FEAST FOR THE EYES

Chef Curtis Rhodes brings to you his cuisine and expertise in this superb Mediterranean restaurant with a contemporary edge. Experience ultimate beauty in this landmark indoor/outdoor restaurant surrounded by lush beautiful gardens and a limestone pond with a three-tiered waterfall cascade. The stage is set for an intimate romantic hideaway. Relax and choose from a selection of crafty libations and a list of more than eighty artisanal wines while ordering one of the luscious, edgy Mediterranean dishes.

You can also sit inside among the bronze-and-wood luxurious décor or enjoy that garden!

5808 NE 4th Court, Miami
305-953-7850

TIP
Sunday brunches are magical. The savory duck hash browns are unforgettable.

• •

DINE IN PARIS
AT LA FRESA FRANCESA

Translation: "The French Strawberry." This petite café/bistro is run by a husband and wife team. It is the hottest French restaurant in town and a true gem in the City of Hialeah. The quaint French décor with vaulted wood ceilings and hanging bulbs and chandeliers take you to a corner of Montmartre. French love songs play as you sip finely paired wines or a guava Bellini. As for the fare, everything is homemade and very French, yet influenced by Miami's own culture. A constant on the menu are crepes and croques. The baked cheeses with honey are great starters. Daily specials include duck, oxtail, quail, and lamb shank. The sauces are superb. Save room for desserts. The decadent Mascarpone Cheese Pie with guava and papaya glaze seals the adventure.

59 West 3rd St., Hialeah
786-717-6886

EXPERIENCE A CARIBBEAN EXPLOSION!
AT ORTANIQUE

Chef Cindy Hutson brings her the flavors of the tropics to our table with her award-winning "Cuisine of the Sun" in this family-owned Caribbean fine cookery restaurant with a charming but elegant island décor. It has been featured on Zagat's Top 10 List of Best Restaurants in Miami ("Extraordinary") for more than fourteen years. Choose from fruity to spicy with everything in between. Their jerk penne pasta with chicken or shrimp brings a light fusion of flavors truly Miami and worthy of its many accolades. Soups and specials change daily. Sit outside for lunch in the quaint sidewalk bistro or walk inside to a spacious and colorful tropical ambiance. Don't forget to try their famed bouillabaisse!

278 Miracle Mile, Coral Gables
305-446-7710

TIP
Appetizers include favorite conch fritters.

ENJOY THE BEST BITE IN MIAMI
AT CHEF ADRIANNE'S

A memorable meal. A memorable experience. It's that bite and that night against which you'll compare all others. Chef Adrianne Calvo has traveled the country and the world in search of adventure, inspiration, and flavors that she can maximize and make her own. Her quaint space in Southwest Miami is nestled in an unassuming shopping center, but inside romantic candles are lit, red roses adorn every table, and every dish is carefully and artfully prepared by the Celebrity Chef herself. She even signs the dishes with her signature "A." She'd probably roll her eyes playfully at the title "Celebrity Chef," but when you've cooked alongside the best chefs in the world on national platforms, such as Food Network's *Chopped* and *Beat Bobby Flay*, you've certainly earned that title. The best ingredients combined with creativity and "maximum flavor" serve up an unforgettable evening for you and that special person.

11510 SW 147th Ave., Miami, 305-408-8386
chefadriannes.com, @ChefAdrianne

TIP
Chef Adrianne was the first chef to bring Dark Dining to Miami. Once a month she hosts a themed Dark Dining event,. You'll touch, hear, smell, and taste the food, which is as amazing as it sounds!

DIVE INTO THE ULTIMATE CUBAN EXPERIENCE
AT VERSAILLES

Versailles, which opened in 1971, is known for lively political conversation about all things Cuban. The food is always fabulous, but we recommend the experience of the *café* (KA-fey), sipped by *la ventanita*, "the window." Every presidential candidate is said to have stopped in for a *cafecito* so that he or she can hear the concerns of the Cuban community. It's the perfect place to gauge public opinion on the hottest issues, which is why it's no surprise to see television crews set up in the parking lot. Celebrities have been known to pop in, too, with everyone from Madonna to Flea, the bassist from the Red Hot Chili Peppers. They go to have their famous "Palomilla Steak" or arroz con pollo.

3555 SW 8th St., Miami
305-444-0240
versaillesrestaurant.com
Family friendly

TIP
Visit La ventanita at Versailles.

REVEL
IN LA MAR PERUVIAN

Located in upscale Brickell Key at the Mandarin Oriental, now you can revel in authentic Peruvian gastronomy with an Asian fusion and upscale novo-Andean fare while enjoying a panoramic ocean view.

Brought to you by acclaimed chef Gaston Acurio, who owns world-renowned Astrid & Gaston, La Mar (Lima), and Tanta, we can taste his signature ceviches and their famed lomo saltado among dozens of famous recipes. Sit outside in the terrace and enjoy a view of the Miami skyline or be comfortable in the cool indoor dining room. Everything about this place is authentic and memorable. Ask about their native Andean wind musicians who often play during brunch on special dates.

500 Brickell Key Dr., Miami
305-913-8358

TIP
Try their sumptuous brunch and enjoy the best pisco sour in town.

PULL UP A CHAIR
AT FINKA TABLE AND TAP

Find a table or grab a seat on a communal rustic bench. Finka comes from the word "finca," which means farm. This Cuban innovative gastropub with Korean/Peruvian influence is the creation of third-generation Miami restaurateurs with Chef Eileen Andrade at the helm. This young chef continues to evolve the Cuban flavors that she grew up with to reflect Miami's cultural palate, and the restaurant has slowly become a favorite among the better Cuban cuisine locales. Don't for get to order a craft beer and try the "KFC," Korean fried chicken. Bibimbap bowls are a favorite too. Located in west Miami-Dade, it's a longer drive but worth it.

14690 SW 26th St., Miami
305-227-8818
finkarestaurant.com

ENJOY A CLASSIC CUBAN MEAL
AT ISLAS CANARIAS

Enjoy family recipes brought over from Cuba. Family-owned Islas Canarias brings you Cuban food at its best, and their dining room is like feasting with the family from the minute you arrive and are greeted by their friendly servers. Topping the list are their famous "Croquetas." These are ham croquettes expertly prepared and fried. Miamians drive from all over to eat them. Savor such dishes as tamal en cazuela (kind of a Cuban Polenta), ajiaco, (hearty soup made with potato-root veggies, corn, and meats), and rabo encendido (oxtail). If you want a quick bite, you can try their mouthwatering "frita," which is a Cuban hamburger. The menu is extensive, so bring an appetite and pack up the leftovers. They also have a drive-through.

13695 SW 26th St., Miami
305-559-6666

TIP
Stop by Islas Canarias Bakery, a few blocks away.

SAVOR ARGENTINE FINE DINING
AT GRAZIANO

Argentines are known for their fabulous meats and pasta dishes, and Graziano tops the list. For years, the Graziano family in Miami has offered the same succulent meats, homemade pastas, and mouthwatering desserts.

Their slow-cooked sumptuous *Parrilla* meats are on display when you enter. Expect to see lamb, pork, and the best meat and rib cuts sizzling on their legendary wood-fired grill to awaken your appetite. Their fine collection of imported Argentinian wines are offered at reasonable prices. Be sure to stop by their market/bakery next door and stock up on a great selection of Argentinian Mendoza region highly rated wines and original delicacies, such as *alfajores*, which is creamy milk caramel sandwiched between two crisp and buttery shortbread cookies.

9227 SW 40th St., Miami, 305-225-0008
grazianosgroup.com, @Grazianos_group

TIP
Take a selfie by the open parilla grill.

Check-out their restaurant and market locations throughout the city and pick-up freshly baked Argentine "empanadas" and sweet delicacies.

GRAZIANO'S RESTAURANTS

Graziano's Bird Road
9227 Bird Rd., Miami

Graziano's in Brickell
177 SW 7th St., Miami
305-860-1426

Graziano's in Coral Gables
394 Giralda Ave., Coral Gables

Graziano's in Hialeah
5993 W 16th Ave., Hialeah

GRAZIANO'S MARKETS

Graziano's in Bird Road Market
3922 SW 92nd Ave., Miami

Graziano's in Coral Gables Market
2301 Galiano St., Coral Gables

Graziano's in Doral Market
11421 NW 41 St., Doral

Graziano's in Hialeah Market
5999 W 16 Ave., Hialeah

Graziano's in Weston Market
1717 Main St., Weston

SAMPLE AUTHENTIC HAITIAN CUISINE
AT TAP TAP

Having the largest Haitian population in the nation, we get the bragging rights. You'll fall in love with this place and its neighborhood vibe the minute you walk in. The blast of colors and beautiful Haitian murals are surpassed only by the mouthwatering food. Savor a modern interpretation of Haiti's classical dishes that are among the best food for your money. Taste their whole fried fish, fried pork chunks, and goat stew, which are spectacular. Servings are ample, but make room for some of the sides and get an order of the *pikliz* (a spicy condiment of peppers, cabbage, shredded carrot, cloves, garlic, and salt) to eat with these dishes. A must eatery.

819 5th St., Miami Beach
305-672-2898
taptapmiamibeach.com

TIP
Don't forget the Mojito.

ENJOY A MAGICAL MEAL
AT THE RUSTY PELICAN

Undisputedly, the best view in town! Surrounded by water, the Miami skyline, and Miami Beach's luxury waterfront star mansions, this iconic, stylish restaurant has been completely updated to a refreshingly eclectic décor, and the food is better than ever before. If you grab an outside table, it's a magical night, but the wall-to-wall glass dining rooms allow you to enjoy the same view if the weather is an issue. A favorite horizon view of downtown Miami. If you want to rediscover contemporary American cuisine and taste fresh local seafood, do it with a Miami twist and add the gorgeous view. Doesn't get any better!

3201 Rickenbacker Causeway, Key Biscayne
rustypelican.com
#therustypelicanmiami

TIP
Don't miss the award-winning brunch. A local seafood feast!

ENJOY COOL AND CASUAL DINING
AT MONTY'S RAW BAR

Everyone dreams about sitting under a tiki hut enjoying an ocean view. This one is the fabulous view of the Coconut Grove Marina. Go in shorts or casual chic, as this outdoor restaurant located in the tropical bohemian neighborhood of Coconut Grove is known for its eclectic mix of artists, adventurers, and intellectuals. Start off with one of their scrumptious soups and then dig into their mouthwatering stone crabs. New on the menu are the Baja tacos and jumbo lump crab cakes. Room for dessert? You can finish off with Monty's local key lime pie, a Florida Keys recipe from Monty's momma.

Happy hour: weekdays 4:00 p.m. to 8:00 p.m. with all drinks discounted. $1 oysters, clams, and shrimp.

2550 S. Bayshore Dr., Miami
305-865-3992
#montysrawbar

TIP
Live music most evenings!

GET TRENDY ROOFTOP DINING
AT JUVIA ON THE BEACH

There's a magical feeling when you sit on a rooftop and gaze at the stars, especially when you are enjoying good food. A delicious fusion of Asian, French, and South American flavors is served up at this eclectic space atop a parking garage with a gorgeous view of the beach, but this is no ordinary building. It is the creation of Swiss designers Jacques Herzog and Pierre de Meuron, and its ultramodern dining with nature is the main attraction. Ceviches, cruditos, cold-smoked scallops, and bonito flakes are part of their innovative cuisine. Ever heard of diamond-hard binchotan coals? Try the beef tenderloin and delight your palate.

1111 Lincoln Rd., Miami Beach
305-763-8272
juviamiami.com
#juviamiami

TIP
Ideal for sunset cocktails.

HAVE A TASTE OF ITALY
AT IL GABBIANO

The winning combination? An Italian trio of chef/entrepreneurs that set out to create magic again. Il Gabbiano is located in the east tower of downtown's One Miami Building. Originally from Abruzzi, Italy, the trio came by way of Los Angeles as owners of Greenwich Village's renowned Il Mulino. With a romantic view of Biscayne Bay as a backdrop, you can relax in the stunning waterfront terrace to enjoy mouthwatering traditional Italian food and freshly made pasta of the day. Porcini ravioli in champagne and black truffle flakes, veal saltimboca, and osso buco are among the many creations. Every detail is executed to perfection to ensure that you have an unforgettable night. A complimentary limoncello completes the experience.

335 Biscayne Blvd., Miami
305-373-0063
ilgabbianomia.com

ENJOY THE VIEW AND SUCCULENT FOOD
AT THE EPIC HOTEL

Unique and breathtaking! Take in the beauty at this seafood restaurant when you go up to the sixteenth floor of 2016 Conde Nast's #1 Rated Hotel in Miami, The Epic. A panoramic view of the glittering waters of Biscayne Bay and the city skyline are second to none. The outdoor lounge is spectacular, and its happy hour has become the hot spot of downtown Miami. Area 31 has rapidly gained its reputation as a top sustainable fishery destination among the pescetarians in town and houses an amazing on-site herb garden on the terrace that provides the fresh ingredients used in the kitchen. Many of the items change daily depending on what chefs find at local farms. Try their crispy octopus and yellowfin tuna, as they are excellent starters, although the Southern flounder and coconut rice steal the show. This place has elevated Miami to a new level of sustainability awareness while dishing up the most exquisite fare.

270 Biscayne Blvd., Miami
305-424-5234
area31restaurant.com

TIP
Every Thursday is Sunset Social, with $8 drinks.

ORDER THE SHRIMP
AT LA CAMARONERA

Whether you ask for a table or eat at the stand-up counter, you will enjoy the succulent fried shrimp. La Camaronera has been featured on Guy Fieri's *Diners, Drive Ins and Dives* and has twice made the *Miami New Times*' "Best of Miami" issue, most recently in 2014. The quality of the seafood at this restaurant is clearly top shelf. Owned by the Garcia family, who were fishermen in Cuba, this is one of their two award-winning fisheries. The family works the counters while they watch the whole flash-fried snapper or fish sandwich piled high with onions go fast. From conch fritters to stone crab and lobster, the food is "fresh, delicious, and simply amazing."

1952 W. Flagler St., Miami
lacamaronera.com
#lacamaronera

TIP
Cash only.

TRY A CUBAN BURGER
AT EL REY DE LAS FRITAS

The Cuban frita typically doesn't need all the fixings, sauces, or even cheese (unless you want it). It's a mouthful of flavor in itself, as this burger meat contains chorizo, chuck, and savory spices. They are bite-size sliders, so you should order two. They come topped with shoestring fried potatoes. If you have a sweet tooth, order the frita dulce, which are chunks of sweet plantains piled on top of the potatoes and chopped onions. Pair it with one of their yummy milk shakes and you have a royal meal. El Rey de las Fritas is just that—king of the fritas. For years they have been dishing up the best fritas in town at several locations.

Original location Little Havana
1821 SW 8th St., Miami
305-644-6054
For additional locations, go to elreydelasfritas.com

SAMPLE AUTHENTIC CUBAN CUISINE
AT EL PALACIO DE LOS JUGOS

Don't let the name fool you. It started out in 1977 at the Flagler Street location, with local and native tropical fruits, and traditional Cuban food was later added to the menu. The open-air concept remained, and the signature vibrant yellow-and-red awning became iconic. With about a dozen locations throughout the city, this is where you find everything Cuban—from all the ingredients to prepare the dish to the ready-to-eat or take-out meals and typical desserts, such as flan, dulce de leche, and arroz con leche. The renowned *lechón* (whole pork cooked in a pit) is always a best-seller as are hog feet, oxtail, tamal en cazuela (cornmeal casserole with meat), soup, and beans. You can feed the whole family with hearty no-frill vittles at a low price.

Original location:
5721 W. Flagler St., Miami
786-631-3733

TIP
Every type of fruit you can imagine.
Try the unique "Mamey" juice.

SAMPLE AWARD-WINNING BITES
AT JUNIOR'S GOURMET BURGER

Beating dozens of national haute cuisine chefs, this burger joint in Miami Springs won the coveted Burger Bash at the South Beach Wine & Food Festival. Since then, owner Junior de la Torre has worn a red silk heavyweight boxing robe to tend his shop, and the lines don't stop all day. Burger Brawl Champs and Best of Miami 2011, Jr's continues to dish up mouthwatering simple food. The gourmet one-third-pound Angus patties fly off the grill with innovative toppings, such as porcini, shitake and oyster mushrooms, sweet ham, and agave lime sauce. Try the platter of three with the incredible home fries. The sweet potato fries are a perfect match too.

7 Westward Dr., Miami Springs
786-360-5347
jrsburgers.com

FIND FANCY SEAFOOD IN A DINING CAR
AT LE MIGNONETTE SEAFOOD AND OYSTER BAR

It's a 1930s gas station turned into an oyster bar! Only in Miami . . . Le Mignonette has the best oyster menu in town. They come from the East Coast and the West Coast as you can read in the large marquee displayed above the bar. Every type of oyster is prepared any way you want. Savor the Caviar Russe's complete line of Michelin Starred Caviar. Order crudos and gourmet specialties that will delight you, but the innovative entries in the "fancy" section of the menu will make you drool. The "Fancy Mignonette Tower" is a towering feast of oysters, clams, snow crabs, shrimp, and crab served atop a half Maine lobster (over $100). Smaller appetite? Try the fish with carrot puree or lobster roll in the menu. Word has it that their bouillabaisse is the best in town!! Still room for more deliciousness? Dig into their homemade blueberry cream cheese pie a la mode.

210 NE 18th St., Midtown, Miami
305-374-4635

COMMIT TO A DIFFERENT WAY OF EATING
AT GLAM

True to their namesake Green Living Animals Matter, GLAM is a fast-casual, plant-based (as in plant-based protein) restaurant in Midtown that has recently opened and taken over the vegan and plant-based eating crowd. The décor is charming and minimalistic. Chef Todd Erickson has brought his expertise from Seed Food and Wine Festival events, and his veggie burger was named Seed's best plant-based burger. The menu is loaded with innovative and elevated plant-based specialties. Such dishes as jackfruit taco al pastor, spaghetti and meatless balls, and farro risotto can be paired with their vegan wines, or you can go for one of their exotic milk shakes. Be sure to leave room for their decadent desserts!

3301 NE 1st Ave., Suite 103-1, Miami
786-864-0590
glam-vegan.com

HANG OUT ON THE RIVER
AT THE WHARF

Take in a 360-degree view of Miami's districts from this open-air pop-up event space right on the historic Miami River. Pop in for brunch weekends and take a taste of Miami's best food trucks offering eclectic high-end bites, such as Cracked by Chef Adrianne's, or take a seat by one of the bars while listening to live music and taking in the view of the Miami River. You're blocks from Downtown Miami and Brickell, so it's a great place to start or end your evening! Come with your children and fur kids with four legs (your dogs) on a leash before 5:00 p.m. on weekends.

Did you know? Expect to see The Wharf evolve and expand, as the City of Miami hopes to add to this riverside spot.

114 SW North River Dr., Miami
305-906-4000
wharfmiami.com
@whartmiami

GET LUCKY
AT 1-800-LUCKY

Like Asian cuisine? Well, you must check out this space! 1-800-LUCKY is an Asian food hall that boasts several options for Asian cuisine—from wok classics to poke bowls, sushi, fried rice, and ramen. Locals who frequent Wynwood will agree that 1-800-LUCKY added a cool, hip vibe to the area, something that we didn't know was missing until we had it! Especially once you've had taiyaki ice cream. It's a feast for the eyes and will likely get lots of "likes" once you post to social because of its unique look. What do you think about a fish-shaped, freshly made waffle cone? Don't think twice about having it. It's really good and melts really fast in the Miami heat, so eat up!

There's plenty of seating in the ten-thousand-square-foot space with limitless options, so don't be intimidated by the crowd of foodies flocking for food! The story starts when you get there. You'll enter through a record store called Lucky Records, which is an experience on its own. Check out cool vinyls, listen to live music, and browse through a small shop that sells everything from snacks to lottery tickets. You'll be texting your friends to visit this cool space the next time they're in Miami.

143 NW 23rd St., Miami
@1800lucky

INDULGE YOUR SWEET TOOTH
AT THE SALTY DONUT

Please "do-nut" be frightened by the long lines outside this donut shop. It merely means you are moments away from sweet greatness—or in this case, salty greatness! The Salty Donut & Coffee Bar serves up the most unique and adventurous flavors in a donut. All donuts here are masterfully created with the best ingredients and made in house, which means when they're out, they are out! They also get bragging rights for coffee with rotating roasts for you to pair with your sweets. There are donuts, and then there are craft donuts. There is a difference. Come taste for yourself!

50 NW 24th St., #112, Miami
305-925-8126
thesaltydonut.com
@thesaltydonut

TIP
The Maple Bacon donut is on their year-round menu, and it's worth trying just for the "bacon cracklings" on top from local smokehouse Miami Smokers.

FIND THE BEST KEY LIME PIE WITHOUT HEADING TO THE KEYS
AT FIREMAN DEREK'S

They're the hottest pies in town, baked by a real-life hero, a City of Miami firefighter. Fireman Derek Kaplan would work his twenty-four-hour shift and then work again on his days off baking pies. Fireman Derek would sell his now famous pies every week on a street corner in Miami. Fireman Derek's Bake Shop & Cafe is packed on any given day with lovers of all things gooey, sweet, and savory. Beyond his perfect pies, his cheesecakes are also amazing. Most people would think that the place to dig into an amazing Key lime pie is in the Florida Keys, and we're not saying the Keys aren't awesome, because they are, but we're just saying that any Key lime pie you'll ever have you will compare to Fireman Derek's Key lime pie. It's simply amazing. We can't recommend one pie over another because this is one of few places where every pie, cake, and cookie you'll taste is just amazing. On a diet? Check it at the door. The calories are worth it!

2818 N Miami Ave., Miami
786-703-3623
firemandereks.com
@fdpies

COME OUT
TO NIGHT OWL COOKIES

You can take a taste of Miami in the culture, art, and music—but what about actually taking a taste of Miami? Come to Night Owl Cookie, and order the Ave Maria. There's your sample of our sweet side in the 305. Guava dough, white chocolate chips, and Maria cookie crumbles. Maria crackers are in most *abuelas'* (grandmothers') handbags. These cookies are carefully crafted, imperfectly round, warm, and stuffed with some kind of gooey goodness. What started out as baking out of his mom's kitchen in 2013 and making deliveries after hours has turned into a super sweet cookie concierge! You see, Night Owl Cookie owner Andrew Gonzalez found himself craving an extra kick late night—he figured he couldn't be the only one! Now, the largest cookie shop in the entire country calls Miami home and bakes about thirty thousand cookies a week in this sweet space, with fifty different rotating flavors late at night! Stop by the shop after 2 p.m. and gaze at all their cookie glory for yourself, take a seat in the one-thousand-square-foot cookie cafe into the early morning hours, and order doorstep delivery online.

10534 SW 8th St., Miami
786-282-7864
nightowlcookieco.com
@nightowlcookies

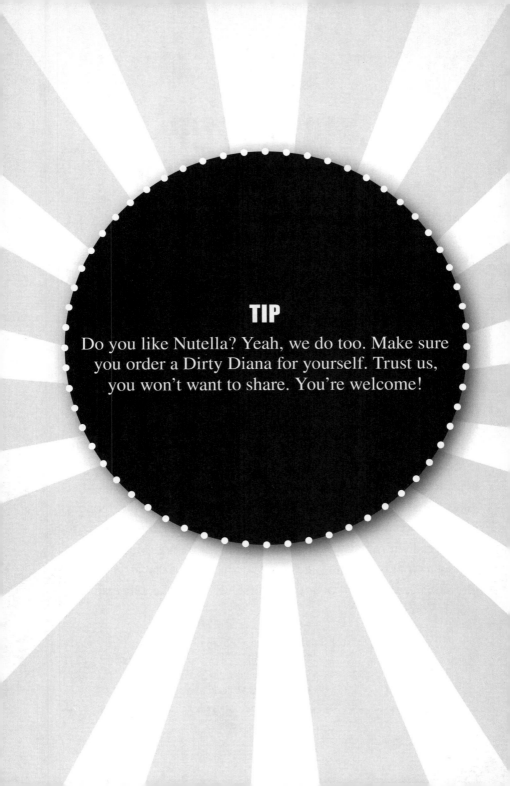

TIP

Do you like Nutella? Yeah, we do too. Make sure you order a Dirty Diana for yourself. Trust us, you won't want to share. You're welcome!

SHAKE IT UP
AT THIS RETRO SHAKE BAR

There's a milk shake in modern-day Miami . . . and then there's a milk shake in Miami served with some nostalgia. So let's take you back to the '80s in Miami. It just tastes . . . sweeter then! Inside Vicky's House Milkshake Bar, it's always #ThrowbackThursday. Your adventure with chocolate malts and churned ice cream starts when you step through a phone booth—a la the movie *Bill and Ted's Excellent Adventure*—and you're taken back in time when you step through to the other side. Vicky's House is a replica of the owner's mother's house in Miami around the late '80s and '90s. Linoleum floors and flowered wallpaper and the theme continues on the counter with the milk shakes. Their signature shakes celebrate classic films with such menu items as E.T. Goes to the Movies to Watch the Goonies (yes, that's the name of the shake!). It's topped with Reese's Pieces and a Baby Ruth bar of course! A shake that pays homage to *The Golden Girls* is all, well, golden—a blondie brownie included and the Breakfast Club shake, yes, like the movie, is adorned with a Salty Donut (see page 42 for more on adding Salty Donut to your bucket list) and comes with a shot of Cuban coffee on the side. Here's a hint: pour the coffee over the shake. Oh yeah. It's good. You're welcome!

3190 Commodore Plaza, Coconut Grove
305-442-3377
vickyshouse.com
@vickyshousebylokal

FIND LOCAL FLAVORS
AT AZUCAR ICE CREAM COMPANY

It became the famous catch phrase of the late, great *Reina de la Salsa*, or "Queen of Salsa," Celia Cruz: ¡*Azucar*! Sugar, that's all it translates to, but sugar means more to Cubans than just having a place in the pantry. *Azucar*, or "sugar," sweetens up our Cuban café and adds a layer of cultural sweetness to this famous ice cream shop that serves up a taste of Miami in an ice cream scoop.

Miami natives could not survive the heat without an abundance of ice cream shops, but Azucar is 305 at its max. Only here can you find local flavors, such as mamey, *plátanos maduro* (sweet plantain). Their most famous flavor is "Abuela María," a rich, creamy vanilla ice cream with ripe guava, chunks of cream cheese, and crushed Maria cookies. Zagat rates Azucar a 4.5 and calls it "fun" and "funky," from the facade to the floors. Ideal for the whole family! As Celia would say . . . ¡*Azucar*!

1503 SW 8th St., Miami
305-381-0369

GO *TAPENADO*
AT TAPAS Y VINOS

For those of you who are new to the tapas culture, the definition of tapas is "small Spanish savory dishes, typically served with drinks at a bar." And Miami is the place to experience this culinary happy time.

Most of the Spanish restaurants transform into tapas hour after 5:00 p.m. These rich appetizer portions of Spanish hams, cheeses, chorizos, stuffed piquillo peppers, seafood delicacies, and much more are served hot or cold. Miamians have faithfully embraced many Spanish traditions, and this one tops the list. So whether at the beach or throughout the city, do what the locals do: Go *tapeando* to some of our favorites:

Casa Juancho
The minute you enter the elegant house of Casa Juancho you forget it's Miami. Authentic brick décor. Spanish pottery and fabric. Hailed as one of Miami's best Spanish restaurants, it was the pioneer of the afternoon tapas.

2436 SW 8th St., Miami
305-642-2452
casajuancho.com

El Carajo Tapas and Wine

Located behind a gas station, this is a true and unique tapas bar. Everything authentic. Served in tablas.

2465 SW 17th Ave., Miami
305-856-2424
el-carajo.com

Diego's

Festive ambience with live piano and performers in truly Iberian mood. Early bird $5 tapas. Charming and fun!

4825 SW 8th St., Miami
305-456-8130

La Taberna de San Roman

Awesome tapas hour with a classy setting in the City of Doral. Look for Flamenco nights.

7800 SW 25th St., Doral
305-593-8110
latabernadesanroman.com

Tapas y Tintos

In the authentic and historic streets of Española Way in Miami Beach. Live entertainment and dancing.

448 Espanola Way, Miami Beach
305-538-8272
tapasytintos.com

RAISE A GLASS

There is so much to celebrate in life, and we're so happy you're celebrating here in Miami! Whether it's bubbly or a locally brewed beer, an exotic red or refreshing rosé, there are so many spots for you to raise a glass in Miami! Here are some sweet spaces some locals might call "secret spots" that we're letting you in on, and other spots you've probably already heard of. Here's your chance to sip and savor them all for yourself! ¡Salud!

Lagniappe
Okay, the pronunciation is tricky, so say it with me. LA-ni-app. There ya go! Don't worry, there won't be a test, but you will want to take notes on the delicious wines you'll discover here! It's a cool and quaint space that will make you feel like you've been swept away to a corner of New Orleans, or Spain even. Lagniappe is open every day, and has live music every day too. There's a huge assortment of wines from all over the world—over 150 different kinds to uncork!

3425 NE 2nd Ave., Miami, 305-576-0108, @laniappe_house

Nancy
A nautical-inspired theme inside, this bar, Nancy, drops anchor in historic Little Havana. *Nancy* was the name of a Revolutionary War ship; it's bartenders have set sail here to mix up creative cocktails or the classics.

2007 SW 8th St., Miami, nancy305.com, @barnancymiam

The Bend Liquor Lounge
There's nothing fancy or swanky here, just good drinks among great people at a price you'll love. The Bend is a dive bar in an older part of Miami Lakes, bordering Hialeah. Secretly tucked away in a strip mall with a somewhat hidden side door entrance by the outdoor seating.

6844 NW 169th St., Miami, 786-542-1948, @thebendmiami

Schnebly Redland's Winery and Brewery

They make wine out of grapes, so why not other tropical fruits you'll only find in South Florida? It's off the beaten path and the southernmost winery in the country. It combines so much of what we love about South Florida and pours all that flavor out of a bottle of delicious vino and beer brewed here too.

30205 SW 217 Ave., Homestead, schneblywinery.com, @schneblywinery

M.I.A. Beer Company

The labels look like Miami, and this beer tastes like Miami—cool, creative and cultural. M.I.A. Beer Company is a craft brewery and taproom with a passion for brewing different flavors of beer, inspired by Miami. Enjoy the more than 50 beers on tap and food in the taproom.

10400 NW 33rd St., Suite 150, Doral, 786-801-1721
mia.beer, @miabeerco

Happy Wine

A mom and pop place run by regular people who just want you...well, they just want you to be happy! Walk in, talk to helpful people, find the wine you're looking for or a new one to try, buy it and if you want, pull up a stool to the wine barrels that serve as a table and enjoy your wine right there after paying an uncorking fee.

Happy Wine Coconut Grove, 2833 Bird Ave., Miami, 305-460-9939

Happy Wine Calle Ocho, 5792 SW 8th St., Miami, 305-262-2465
happywinemiami.com, @happywinemiami

Wynwood Brewing Company

Locals were so excited about Wynwood Brewing Company in the heart of Wynwood, the first craft brewery to open there. Operating a 15-barrel brewhouse, they serve their bold beers for you to try in their tap room and are distributed all over South Florida and beyond.

565 NW 24th St., Miami, 305-982-8732, @wynwoodbrewing

The Tank Brewing Co.

The taproom offers 16 taps and an opportunity to meet the team and see the process happens in the 25,000 square feet of space. Come with a big crowd; it can certainly accommodate a big group of friends or a quaint date night. Check out the fun games around for some throwback fun!

5100 NW 72nd Ave., Bay A1, Miami, 786-801-1554, @thetankbrewing

MUSIC AND ENTERTAINMENT

LIVE IT UP
AT LIV

The vibrations will pulse through you, the beat pumps along with your heart, the laser lights will be your dancing partner here. When you hear stories about the exhilarating nightlife in Miami, you can likely trace that story back to LIV nightclub inside the historic Fontainebleau Miami Beach. This electric space has redefined the nightlife experience in Miami. Welcoming top entertainers from around the world, the LIV experience sets you up for an unforgettable night. The space itself is incredible. Artful architecture and technology fill the more than eighteen thousand square feet of space that comes to life when you walk through and the music from world-famous DJs and artist fills the room. The energy is contagious and fun. Keep your eyes peeled for celebrities at the VIP tables. This is where they party!

4441 Collins Ave., Miami
305-674-4680
livnightclub.com
@livmiami

TIP
The dress code is enforced, so dress to impress!

INDULGE IN NOSTALGIA
AT HOY COMO AYER

Please don't leave Miami without crossing this experience off your bucket list. "Hoy Como Ayer" translates to "Today, Just Like Yesterday." This space is profoundly nostalgic, with every corner thoughtfully and proudly evoking Cuba circa 1950. Wood paneling and a rustic-looking bar with images of the greatest voices that ever sang don the walls here. Some of those voices have performed on this stage to a packed dance floor. If you're looking for a night of salsa dancing where you can really take in the Cuban culture, come here. If you like jazz, come here. If you like well-made mojitos or Cuba Libres (that's a rum and coke) come here. Pair it up with lite bites at a small cafe table tucked away in a corner and let the music and Latin grooves take over your soul.

2212 SW 8th St., Miami
305-5451-2631
@hoycomoayerclub

HEAR THE BEST LIVE LATIN MUSIC
AT BALL & CHAIN

Why do we say the best live Latin music? Because of all the history in this place and how it comes to life when filled with music, food, drinks, and good people. Ball & Chain opened in 1935 during the Depression, which hit hard in most of the country, but the transient city that Miami was and still is fared quite well. Here, there was gambling, liquor laws were violated, and jazz music was played in a pre-Cuban migration Miami in the '30s and '50s. Even though the likes of Billie Holiday played here, its doors were closed after twenty-five years. It was reopened in 2014, and the history resurrected within it. The wallpaper, floor tile, and, yes, the music—Latin music pulses through this space. Ball & Chain pays homage to its history with every cocktail poured, jazz set played, and late-night pachanga that roars of Cuban big band, making you move all night!

1513 SW 8th St., Little Havana
ballandchainmiami.com
@ballandchainMIA

TIP

All that dancing making you hungry?
There is a delicious menu to enjoy here too!
Check out their website or social media pages
for free salsa lessons on some nights!

DANCE
AT ESTEFAN KITCHEN

They are humble, kind, and as warm and loving as any people you'll meet, but make no mistake—they are legends. Gloria Estefan and Emilio Estefan broke down barriers before the phrase "breaking barriers" was even used. They each fled their homeland of Cuba, and their story is the story of the human spirit and hunger for the American dream. That's why they came to this country and why they came to Miami. The Grammy award–winners held on to their Cuban roots. Miami is their home. Their roots are here now, and you can taste it.

Estefan Kitchen, in the heart of the Miami Design District, has extra spice and sound. Their namesake restaurant offers a sophisticated take on Cuban classics, both food and beverage. Instruments are set up on a small stage by the bar, and you never know who will come up to play. Sometimes it's the talented servers and staff, and sometimes it's Emilio Estefan himself. Musicians play here, you dance here, and just outside the beautiful stage and in the courtyard surrounded by shops, you have the Palm Court. Emilio Estefan has produced shows and brought in award- winning performers who play for packed crowds. The Palm Court Performance Series has welcomed Il Volo, Arturo Sandoval, and Emily Estefan, whose voice soars and sings her own incredible story.

140 NE 39th St., #133, Miami, estefankitchen.com, @estefankitchen

GET COZY AND COOL
AT THE YARD

The Wynwood Yard is another of Miami's biggest success stories. Locals love Wynwood, and visitors love to check it out. It's unpretentious, inspirational, and at every turn there's good food and drinks here! All that comes together at the Wynwood Yard. Imagine a large open green space in the middle of the art district in Miami. There's an open-air bar right in the middle, a quaint stage for performances, and several food trucks, container restaurants, and stores all around. Welcome to Wynwood Yard—truly a gift—a magical space created for you. This space is child friendly, too, so a fun and hip night can be enjoyed by everyone!

56 NW 29th St., Miami
@wynwoodyard

LET'S HANG OUT
AT EL PATIO

The translation for El Patio is the "backyard," and that's exactly what this cool spot looks and feels like! This isn't a place to check out for a lavish, over-the-top nightclub experience. You come here for a raw and rugged night of dancing and fun and what feels like a Latin pub. Visit El Patio in the afternoon. Sit down, have a drink, and catch up over bar bites, such as tequeños, which are Venezuelan-style cheese sticks, or pulled pork sliders. Show up later at night and get ready to dance when it gets loud and packed! There is an indoor space, part of the outside is covered, and most is open-air playing Pacific vibes, cumbia funk, reggaeton, and more. Look out for a cover on Friday and Saturday nights.

167 NW 23rd St., Miami
elpatiowynwood.com
@elpatiowynwood

SEE A SHOW
AT EL TUCAN, A SWANKY SUPPER CLUB

El Tucan Nightclub is beautiful. The scene is set for an experience that evokes the glitzy glamour of a Cuban cabaret mixed with Miami's sparkle in a Great Gatsby kind of way. Celebrate a special occasion or just have an experience here, where you see a burlesque-style show or take in the sounds of an eleven-piece orchestra house band while enjoying lite bites and cocktails. Since opening in Brickell, El Tucan has evolved into a late-night destination. After the curtain goes down on the cabaret show, the club takes over, with live performances and DJs making you move into the early Miami hours.

1111 1st Ave., Miami
305-535-0065
eltucanmiami.com
@eltucanmiami

SEE CULT CLASSICS
AT NITE OWL THEATER

Make your movie night unique while visiting Miami. Nestled in Miami's Design District among high-end stores, you'll find a theater that always celebrates "Throwback Thursday." Nite Owl Theater projects classic films in the most classic way—on 35mm film! Walk in and you're greeted by towering old-school projectors, classic candy, and buttery popcorn. Whether it's creature features with Freddy Krueger or hits from the early '90s, you'll hear the change of film on the projectors and the clicking of the film. At times, the only 35mm copies of the films are here, expertly running through the hands of Nayib Estefan, who strives to keep 35mm alive.

3930 NW 2nd Ave., #201, Miami
niteowltheater.com
@niteowltheater

TIP
There's a bean bag room where movies are projected on the wall, original Nintendo NES to play, and remember the days when it was "kind to rewind"? Yes, there's a secret room where you watch movies on VHS tapes, and kid flicks are here too!

STAY AT THE FAENA

See for yourself why Faena has been named a number one place to stay in the United States.

Wow! Just wow! Practice saying that because that will be your reaction at every turn when you walk into Faena Hotel Miami Beach. It's not a hotel. It's a destination. It's an experience. It's evident from the second you step into the main space at Faena that the minds behind this space are unique. They're risk takers, and they were set to do something different. They did just that in building Faena in Buenos Aires, Argentina, and Miami was next, starting the global expansion for this experience for all to have at least once. The colors of art are deep and rich, the spa is healing, the dining is memorable. Faena Theater sets the stage for performances, and several unique spaces are here for you to enjoy an expertly crafted cocktail. Faena is for the entire family.

For a historic experience, Casa Faena is about two blocks down in the Faena District and across the street from the beach. This is more of a boutique hotel experience, as the building is historic. So you'll feel as if you're staying in a home as opposed to a hotel. It's an awesome opportunity to still admire the "Faena flair," with a nod to Miami's historic Art Deco design and feel.

3201 Collins Ave., Faena District, Miami Beach
Casa Faena, 3500 Collins Ave., Miami Beach
faena.com, @faena

· ·

VISIT
THE FAMOUS FONTAINEBLEAU

With its signature curve, classic black-and-white marble lobby floors, and the legendary "stairway-to-nowhere," Fontainebleau Miami Beach is a landmark. Lose yourself in the 17,000-square-foot lobby and the history of this grand place will speak to you. It opened in 1954 and was an immediate go-to getaway for the biggest names in show business—Elvis Presley, Bob Hope, Lucille Ball, Frank Sinatra. Today, Fontainebleau still has those bragging rights. She still honors her historic past but is dressed in modern design and luxury in the most modest way, but you won't feel intimidated by Fontainebleau's grandeur because she welcomes everyone. The rooms are inviting and comfortable, the poolside cabanas are envy worthy, the spa is luxurious and relaxing, and the dining lip smacking. Award-winning celebrity chefs let themselves be inspired by Miami, her culture, her people, and her beaches are right outside! Start your evening at Sorso by Scott Conant, a preparty to the pasta party at Scarpetta! Steak lovers can enjoy strip steak by Michael Mina, who plates beautiful dishes with meat that melts when you take a bite. Hakkasan serves up Cantonese cuisine that is fresh and exotic. Family getaway or adult getaway, Fontainebleau Miami Beach is a single-stop destination right on the sands of one of the most famous beaches in the world.

4441 Collins Ave., Miami Beach
fontainebleau.com, @fontainebleau, @dinebleau

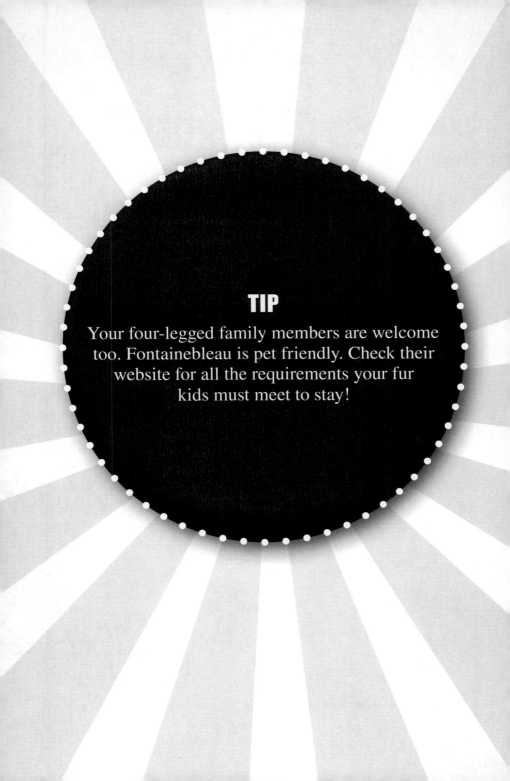

TIP

Your four-legged family members are welcome too. Fontainebleau is pet friendly. Check their website for all the requirements your fur kids must meet to stay!

FIND JAZZ UNDER THE MIAMI MOON
AT THE GARDENS MUSIC FESTIVAL

Once a year the City of Miami Gardens welcomes some of the biggest stars in music. It's a celebration of South Florida's eclectic culture and diversity through art performed on stage. The Jazz in the Gardens Music Festival has welcomed such world-renowned performers as Common, LL Cool J, Smokey Robinson, Chaka Khan, Anita Baker, Salt-N-Peppa, and Kid 'N Play. This annual event continues to evolve the talent on stage while nourishing future talented hopefuls to one day be a part of this awesome event. Jazz in the Gardens offers invaluable networking opportunities to emerging musicians, artists, poets, filmmakers, and more through its FMAC program: Film, Music, Art & Culture, a conference held during this event. It's become a weekend in March that locals look forward to and one that fans and artists from all over set aside to be part of the party.

Takes place at Hard Rock Stadium
347 Don Shula Dr., Miami Gardens
jazzinthegardens.com
@jazzgardens

FIST PUMP ALL NIGHT LONG
AT ULTRA MUSIC FESTIVAL

Imagine the world's premier outdoor electronic music festival. Then imagine the backdrop of the azure-blue waters with the LED light displays glittering in the rippling waters of Biscayne Bay. If electronic dance music is for you, then come to Miami when it hosts the world-renowned Ultra, a three-day EDM music festival that comes annually during the month of March. More than 150,000 attendees pour into the streets of downtown Miami, paralyzing traffic and bringing the eclectic crowd as the vibrations of hardcore electronic music is the fix of the night. Famous EDM DJs, such as Tiesto, David Guetta, Steve Aoki, Afrojack, and Carl Cox, are among the 175 acts and tents.

Bayfront Park
ultramusicfestival.com

STAY AT THE VAGABOND HOTEL,
ANOTHER MIAMI ICON

You're not on Ocean Drive or in Downtown. You're in Miami's MiMo Historic District, and staying at this historic hotel is a great way to see it. It's a 1950s-inspired space refurbished and brought into modern-day Miami but still keeping its charm. MiMo is Miami Modern, the district spanning more than twenty-seven blocks, from NE 50th to NE 77th Streets along Biscayne Boulevard. The City of Miami really started putting love into this once run-down area and has breathed life back into it! Trendy boutiques, cools bars, and restaurants bring fans from all ZIP codes in Miami, but you don't have to go far if you're staying at the Vagabond, known for its Pool Bar and the acclaimed bites served at its restaurant, Vagabond Kitchen and Bar.

7301 Biscayne Blvd., Miami
305-400-8420
@vagabondhotelmiami

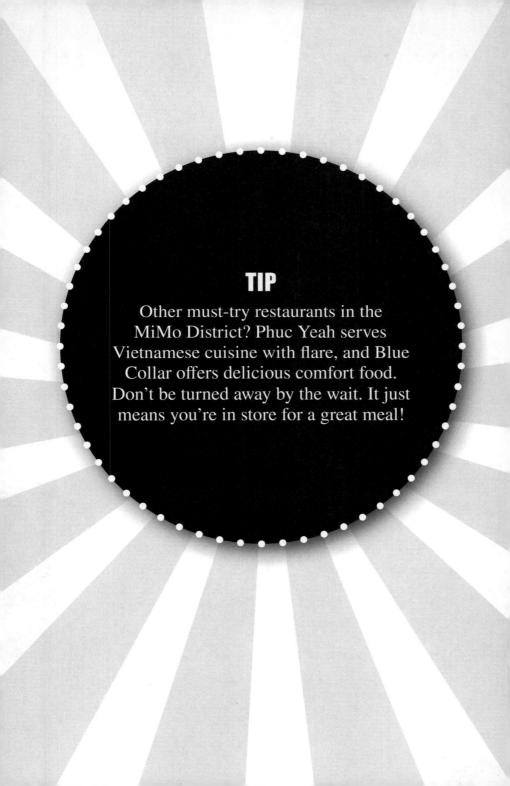

TIP

Other must-try restaurants in the MiMo District? Phuc Yeah serves Vietnamese cuisine with flare, and Blue Collar offers delicious comfort food. Don't be turned away by the wait. It just means you're in store for a great meal!

SURROUND YOURSELF WITH LUXURY
AT THE MIAMI BEACH EDITION

Check out this "Edition" of a one-stop stay in Miami Beach.

It's the perfect fusion of intimacy, luxury, and exclusivity. As you walk into the lobby, you'll be greeted by vivacious music, a sweet scent, white floors, and clusters of candles that'll make you want to redesign your own home modeled after this serene space! It's welcoming, and it's modern, but she honors her historic roots of the Seville Hotel, which opened in 1955 and whose sign still adorns the top of the hotel. Lunch among the lush greenery at Tropicale and take a dip in the originally restored swimming pool. Also snap a selfie by the original dive board there. Lounge in the "sandbox," a sandy hideaway with pillows and hammocks, where movies are screened at night. When the sun goes down, this is the place to get a taste of the best nightlife experience in Miami at the Basement. It's a multidimensional experience, where you can go bowling, don some skates in the rink, and, yes, dance until the next day.

2901 Collins Ave., Miami Beach
786-257-4500
@editionhotels

Inspired by the history of the Seville Hotel and the glamour of its time, world-renowned chef Jean-Georges Vongerichten brings you the iconic Matador Room's lavish menus that offer his fusion of Caribbean, Spanish, Latin, and South American cuisines. The seasonal menus are from the freshest locally sourced seasonal produce, blending the flavors of Miami's multicultural cuisine. The innovative entrees include eggs Benedict served in corn flour tortillas, chipotle chicken tacos, a turkey Cuban sandwich, and arroz con pollo.

Reminiscent of the dazzling supper clubs of the '40s and '50s, the oval dining room greets you with its original and restored hanging chandelier. Or you can go outside to enjoy the luscious green foliage terrace beneath a Brazilian ipe wood trellis with climbing bougainvilleas. A true Miami opulent experience.

2901 Collins Ave., Miami Beach
786-257-4500, @editionhotels

BOOK A LANDMARK,
THE BILTMORE

In the roaring 1920s, champagne flowed, the foxtrot reigned supreme, and golf balls were hit around here; it's not much different in modern-day Miami. The Biltmore continues to host the most lavish events for all its guests and visitors. The Biltmore is almost as known for its 600,000-gallon, 23,000-square-foot pool, still one of the largest pools in the entire country! See how big it is for yourself, play a round of golf on the championship course, relax at the spa, or dine at the award-winning restaurants on site.

This is great getaway for the family to disconnect and reconnect with each other. Locals from all over South Florida plan ahead and make sure they have a room secured at The Biltmore so they can take in the magnificent fireworks display on the Fourth of July holiday. Blankets cover the famous golf course, people of all ages crowd around the pool—and then, just look up! The fireworks paint the sky over the City of Coral Gables for almost an hour—the party is even more extravagant on New Year's Eve.

The Biltmore offers a spectacular spread for brunch on Sundays and traditional English afternoon tea Wednesday through Sunday. Reservations are recommended for either event.

1200 Anastasia Ave., Coral Gables
855-311-6903
@biltmorehotel

SPORTS AND RECREATION

REEL IN
THE MIAMI MARLINS

Experience the energetic baseball culture of Miami in the unforgettable thirty-seven-thousand-seat Marlins Stadium. Its impressive dome has changed the Miami horizon. With its retractable roof, it houses the controversial $2.5 million *Home Run* sculpture by world-renowned artist Red Grooms. It is wild pop art in a Miami-wild baseball culture that has struck a nerve with some and loved by others when its LEDs light up and makes noise. The statue with a cloud backdrop depicts Florida-inspired flair, flora, and fauna. When the Marlins hit a homerun, the pelicans, seagulls, jumping marlins, a pair of flamingos that flap their wings, jetting streams of water, and rolling ocean waves will activate, and it all comes alive.

The Miami Marlins (formerly the Florida Marlins) have won two World Series—in 1997 as the first wild card team to ever win the Championship—and then in 2003, when they stunned the baseball world to defeat the New York Yankees.

Although plagued by managerial changes and injuries, their future is looking good as new co-owner Derek Jeter is expected to turn around the streak of losing seasons. Watch the exciting young team and have some good old Miami fun in this amazing stadium!

Marlins Stadium
501 Marlins Way, Miami
305-480-1300, mlb.com/marlins

TURN UP THE HEAT,
THE MIAMI HEAT

For more than thirty years, Miami has brought the world of basketball to its feet. The Heat's three NBA Championship wins and seventeen playoff appearances have kept them at the top of the basketball world and ranked among the top five. Their home-based, twenty-thousand-seat American Airlines Arena is a top-notch facility that features the latest and greatest of service and accommodations.

The home crowd's energy has been a pivotal factor and the talk of many visiting NBA teams. The arena also houses eighty luxury suites and seventy-six private boxes, but with its Nano Lumens screen displays throughout the patios and the giant façade screen, fans are equally informed of what is going on.

As for transportation, consider UBER, which has become the official ridesharing app of the Heat. The deal includes special drop-off zones and designated entrances. If you enjoy riding the train, the Miami Metrorail and Metro Mover are probably the best way to get there to avoid the parking hassle. They also have ample parking lots and public parking surrounding the arena, with valet parking at a hefty forty dollars per game.

AAA Arena, 601 Biscayne Blvd., Miami
aaarena.com

CHEER
THE MIAMI HURRICANES

There is nothing more thrilling than college ball, and with twenty-one combined sports national championships, the University of Miami Hurricanes bring the thrill and the hometown crowd to its feet. Whenever there's a home game (whether it's football, baseball, or soccer), you can drive down US1 and see the sky lit up for miles, and the roar of the crowds can be heard for blocks. The U, as lovingly referred to by fans of the 'Canes all over the country, were reinvigorated with the athletic program with the introduction of the infamous turnover chain on the football field in 2017. See it for yourself. The thirty-six-inch, ten-karat gold chain with nine hundred orange and green stones to adorn the "U" is pretty hard to miss no matter where your seats are for the football game! The inside sports arenas are also packed with fans and pom-poms. Check out the schedule on their athletics page and be sure to catch the ball fever in town.

University of Miami Canes
1320 S. Dixie Hwy., Coral Gables
hurricanesports.com

EXPERIENCE
THE FIU PANTHERS

FIU has one of the largest student bodies in the nation, and a fierce fan home-based crowd fills the stands and gyms of all their home games, making this a one-of-a-kind, adrenaline-filled, wild experience. As for bragging rights, Florida International University has many. It prides itself on supporting eighteen intercollegiate sports teams called the Panthers. Being a young athletic program, the student athletes, student body, and fans can be a part of the history to be made. They have top-notch sports facilities, and you can find ample parking throughout the campus.

Florida International University Panthers
11200 SW 8th St., Miami
fiusports.com

ATTEND
THE INTERNATIONAL CHAMPIONS CUP

Some call it soccer. Most call it football. Regardless of what you call it, the sport is huge, and Miami has a piece of it! The city has hosted matches in the International Champions Cup several times since 2013. Miami played host to the historic EL Clasico match between Real Madrid and FC Barcelona in 2017, the first time that match was ever been played outside Spain. We continue to welcome the biggest soccer teams in the world as part of the ICC to take over our town, along with the most passionate fans! International soccer star David Beckham also sees that the fans here want more and plans to bring Major League Soccer to Miami.

International Champions Cup
Hard Rock Stadium
347 Don Shula Dr., Miami Gardens
internationalchampionscup.com

EXPLORE DIFFERENT DIMENSIONS OF FUN
AT FUNDIMENSION

This place is fun overload, and you'll love it as much as your children will! This haven for all things happy and fun was created by a mother with children for other families to enjoy. FunDimension in Wynwood offers so much in one place. The air-conditioning is important in South Florida, especially in the hot and humid summer months. Flip out in the Bungy Dome, get lost in Laser Tag, and spin out in the modern, immersive version of bumper cars in the Spin Zone. There's an arcade with games where you get something for winning. There's even a 7-D theatre—an all-immersive eight-seat capsule theater!

Tip: 2129 NW 1st Ct., Miami
786-360-1766
@fundimension

TIP
There's also food to fuel all the energy you and the children will burn off!

GET WILD
AT ZOO MIAMI!

It's hot in Miami, and that's just how many of the amazing animals at Zoo Miami like it! It is the largest and oldest zoological garden in the Sunshine State and the only subtropical zoo in the country. You'll want to rent a group bike to cover the entire zoo and see the hundreds of animals that call Zoo Miami home. The climate here allows the zoo to have animals from Asia, Australia, and Africa. Though Zoo Miami was one of Hurricane Andrew's victims in 1992, more than twenty-five years later it's one of South Florida's greatest success stories and home to more than three thousand animals representing more than five hundred species. See the animals up close, ask experts on hand questions, be sure to see the giraffes, and feed them too!

Did you know? Zoo Miami is an active part of more than thirty-six conservation projects on six continents around the world!

12400 SW 152nd St., Miami
305-251-0400
zoomiami.org
@zoomiami

TAKE IN 360 DEGREES OF OCEAN VIEW
AT SOUTH POINTE PARK

It looks like an art installment, but as you get a little closer and follow the laughter, you'll see a lot of splashing going around! You'll likely already have a bathing suit packed, so make a stop at the splash pad at South Pointe Park. Your children will have so much fun cooling off and taking a stroll on the wide paths along the grassy areas. Take a deep breath and take it all in because you'll get some of the best ocean views in town from South Pointe Park. Keep an eye out for famous faces and photoshoots here too. This one of the most photographed areas on Miami Beach, so snap a selfie!

1 Washington Ave., Miami Beach
305-673-7730
miamiandbeaches.com
@miamiandbeaches

TIP
Besides the tot lot or small playground for children, there's a playground for your fur kids too!

SEE
SEA TURTLES HATCH

It's something you might have read about or seen on television, but there's nothing like seeing the majesty of Mother Nature hatch before you—literally hatch! Did you know that almost 70 percent of sea turtle nesting happens in Florida? It's an opportunity to see something incredible but also a reminder for all of us to be responsible for our actions to keep protecting these amazing creatures and their natural habitats. Pregnant female turtles come back to the very beach they hatched from, find a safe space above the water line, and lay about a hundred eggs. The eggs stay in the sand for about sixty days, and then the magic happens. The baby turtles all hatch at the same time and follow the downward slope of the sand and the light of the moon and stars to the ocean. That's why the beaches are kept dark at night so as not to disorient the hatchlings. Several nature conservation organizations have a mission to protect and preserve sea turtles as well as educate others on the process. See for yourself!

Miami Eco Adventures
miamidade.com/ecoadventures
305-310-3046, 305-666-5885
@miamidadeseaturtles
*Reservations are required

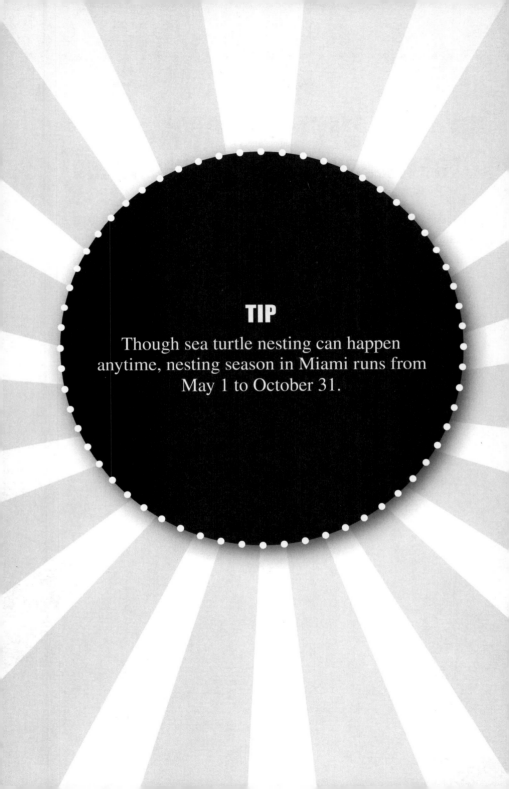

TIP

Though sea turtle nesting can happen anytime, nesting season in Miami runs from May 1 to October 31.

VIEW MIAMI
FROM A PONTOON OR PADDLE BOARD

There's seeing Miami from land, and there's seeing Miami from the water! You should add a water experience to your bucket list. There are so many options for water sports, but if you're not that athletic, relax on a pontoon boat that cruises around Biscayne Bay. See some beautiful homes and stop on deserted islands, where you can have a picnic, or strap yourself into a standup paddle board! You don't have to be a pro to enjoy paddle boarding, and you can even take a calm pet with you for the ride. Check out Miami Beach Paddle and Co. with various options for rentals right across from the Eden Roc hotel in Miami Beach.

4525 Collins Ave., Miami Beach
305-300-1926
beachpaddleco.com
@beachpaddleco

CLIMB WALLS
LIKE A NINJA

The hit show phenomenon *American Ninja Warrior* has helped breed a new hybrid athlete, in which precision, thought, endurance, and strength supersedes any muscle size! You can even take on the wall, yeah, that wall! The obstacle course built inside Ninja Lounge in North Miami was designed by the same minds behind the course you see on the television show! Test your own endurance and grip strength. Beyond just the course, this multidimensional experience will immerse the entire family in a strictly fun zone!

14401 NE 19th Ave., North Miami
785-590-5000
ninjalounge.com
@ninjaloungnorthmiami

SHIFT INTO HIGH GEAR
WITH THE COOLEST CARS IN MIAMI

Are you a car aficionado? This place is more than just a cool car museum. It's pretty over the top, with rides you won't see anywhere else. The Dezer Collection at the Miami Auto Museum is home to the famous Batmobile! The caped crusader parks his car here. Walk into Miami's version of the Batcave and check out Batmobiles from different eras, the Batboat, and the Batcycle too! Kids—and the big kids—will love every moment of the memorabilia on display. This is also home of the world's largest privately held James Bond display. Bond, James Bond, and so many of agent 007's gizmos and gadgets are here. Known for his slick rides, at least one vehicle representing each of the first twenty-three Bond films can be seen here.

14401 NE 19th Ave., North Miami
dezercollection.com
@dezerautomuseum

EXPERIENCE CUBAN CULTURE
IN LITTLE HAVANA

Ahhh, historic Little Havana. Take a walk and let the pulse of this historic site stimulate all your senses. Little Havana is the heartbeat of the Cuban community. Any major event that comes to Miami is sure to get the "signature shot" of the big Cuban cigars and the Cuban coffee sitting cornerside on a domino game table. This is where they come to get that signature shot. Stop by Maximo Gomez Park. Locals simply call it Domino Park, a place where the Cuban exile community comes to throw down a domino game and where visitors snap a picture to get the most "likes" on their posts. Little Havana has evolved into and evolved with Modern Miami. It's a must-see stop that shares the story of any immigrant, with art on display in galleries from all over Latin America, food from all cultures, and Cuban rhythms that play out of every cafe, restaurant, story, and gallery. However, it holds on to its roots, which are celebrated during Viernes Culturales or Cultural Fridays (a monthly cultural festival) on the last Friday of every month between 13th and 17th Avenues on SW 8th Street. Little Havana is also a perfect place to scope out and pick up Cuban memorabilia, smoke a Cuban cigar, and stop at the Tower Theater, one of Miami's oldest landmarks, which opened in 1926 and still shows films for you to enjoy.

Maximo Gomez Park, aka Domino Park
801 SW 15th Ave., Miami

FIND ART IN THE PARK
AT PINECREST GARDENS

It's a walk through paradise. Pinecrest Gardens is one of the most prized experiences in the Village of Pinecrest. It's a beautiful walk with nature and the history of this area, which once was home to different species of birds. Today, a stroll through Pinecrest Gardens will introduce you to more than one thousand different types of exotic plants native to South Florida, but this park is more than just Mother Nature's canvas. It's an Arts Park with exhibits throughout, a gallery, a resident artist, and conservation projects year-round. This is also just a fun place for the family! Reserve a table to play dominoes and pack a picnic lunch or come a little later to see a movie or a concert. Admission to the park's Splash 'N Play is included, which is a perfect spot to cool down on a hot Miami day. Be sure to check out the petting zoo and feed the fish!

11000 Red Rd., Pinecrest
pinecrestgardens.com
@pinecrest_gardens

TIP
Pinecrest Gardens hosts a beautiful farmers market every Sunday year-round! Admission is free!

CRUISE THE BAY,
CHECK OUT MILLIONAIRE'S ROW

Celebrities love having a Miami Beach address. It's a vacation home for some and main residence for many. Now you can find their addresses while enjoying drinks and light snacks aboard the *Island Queen* "Millionaire's Row" Cruise. The ninety-minute narrated tour of Miami's skyline sails through Biscayne Bay, and it's lots of fun. See the cruise ships at the Port of Miami, and visit Fisher Island, home of the Vanderbilts, but the highlight of the cruise are Star, Palm, and Hibiscus Islands, and "Millionaire's Row"—home to such celebrities as Madonna, J.Lo, Shaquille O'Neal, Rosie O'Donnell . . . and the list goes on. Zoom those lenses when you spot them in their luxurious yachts and document the tales you'll be bringing home. You can buy tickets for twenty-seven dollars at Bayside. Once you go through the main entrance, continue to the ocean, where you will find a small booth and the docking site.

Island Queen Cruises
Bayside Marketplace
401 Biscayne Blvd., Miami
305-577-3344
baysidemarketplace.com
@bayside_marketplace

TOUR THE EVERGLADES
IN AN AIRBOAT

Nicknamed "The River of Grass" for the tall, sharp sawgrass that emerges from the water, the Florida Everglades National Park encompasses 1.5 million acres. With two entrances in South Florida and a fee of only twenty-five dollars per vehicle, you can explore its rivers, lakes, marshes, ponds, prairies, and forest of deep mangrove swamps. It's the largest remaining subtropical wilderness in the United States and one of the world's great biological wonders. Climb the sixty-five-foot-tall Shark Valley observation tower, which is just twenty-five miles west of Miami, and marvel in the unobstructed view of eighteen miles of the Everglades' exotic birds, flora, and fauna.

Another way to visit the Everglades is by airboat. More than fifty-six endangered species are protected in this unique environment. Experience the native wildlife up close and enjoy its splendor. Catch an alligator safari and look for the little red eyes. Snap a picture and you'll see the faces of alligators. Airboats accommodate parties of all sizes.

TIP
You might even get to pet a baby alligator.

HERE ARE SOME AIRBOAT TOURS TO CHECK OUT

Tigertail Airboat Tours
17696 Tamiami Trail, Miami
305-439-2745

Coopertown Airboats
22700 Tamiami Trail, Miami
305-226-6048

Gator Park Airboat Tours
24050 Tamiami Trail, Miami
305-559-2255

Everglades Safari Park
26700 Tamiami Trail, Miami

SOAK UP THE SUN
ON OUR WORLD-FAMOUS BEACHES

Did you know that the inventor of suntan lotion was a pharmacist from Miami Beach? His name was Benjamin Green, and in 1944 he came up with the famous potion of cocoa butter and coconut oil and later named it Coppertone. It's a fact that when you think of Miami, the bright sun and its blue oceans come to mind, and that's why tourists flock here every winter. Miami-Dade County stretches along twenty-eight miles of the Atlantic's bluest waters, and going to the beach remains Miamians' main attraction and what makes this city glimmer with energy. Used for photo shoots and movie scenes, Miami Beach remains one of the nation's most filmed and photographed areas. The television show *Miami Vice* made the nation fall in love with our lifestyle, and we have revered it as our own paradise and nature's gift. So take your pick, and if you plan to visit the sun, here are the top picks and a word from the locals.

BEACHES

South Beach and Nikki Beach
People watching, monokinis, model photo shoots, nightlife and dining. It's America's Riviera. Nikki Beach is a celebrity spot. Have your camera ready.

Cape Florida
At Bill Baggs State Park, Key Biscayne. Ranked twice among Forbes top 25 beaches in the country. Family fun, fishing, biking, and boat camping.

Virginia Key
Playground with a miniature train and carousel on the way to Key Biscayne.

Haulover Beach
Where clothing is optional.

Sunny Isles Beach
Ranked #1 of Top Ten U.S. destinations by Trip Advisor.

Hobie Beach
Popular among windsurfers and dog lovers.

South Pointe Park and Beach
With a tot lot and interactive water features, fishing pier, sidewalk jogging, and green areas with shaded palms and trees. Great spot to pose for pics.

CULTURE AND HISTORY

MAKE YOUR WAY
TO THE ADRIENNE ARSHT CENTER
FOR THE PERFORMING ARTS

In Miami's constellation of cultural organizations, Adrienne Arsht Center for the Performing Arts broke ground in 2006 and claimed the city's appetite for cultural diversity. This world-class live performance and visual arts complex is the second-largest performing arts center in the United States and the largest one in Florida. It hosts more than four hundred performances a year and draws more than 450,000 people to Miami's cultural core.

Enjoy the Internationally acclaimed resident companies that perform here: The Florida Grand Opera, The New World Symphony, Broadway Across America, and one of the country's most respected ballet companies in the nation—the Miami City Ballet, which performs at the Ziff Ballet Opera House. Don't miss the world's best flamenco dancing when Ballet Nacional de España comes to Miami during flamenco week.

The Arsht Center for the Performing Arts places Miami as the gateway culture vessel of the Americas. Check out the calendar and plan your visit.

1300 Biscayne Blvd., Miami
305-946-6722
arshtcenter.org

GET DAZZLED
AT ART BASEL

During the first week of December, more than eighty thousand visitors travel thousands of miles to witness the best in modern and contemporary visual arts. Miami Beach rolls out the red carpet as host to the world's most prestigious artists, collectors, curators, and aficionados during Art Basel. Nearly three hundred of the world's premier art galleries display their masterpieces in more than 500,000 square feet of exhibit space.

Miami's landscape transforms to reflect the city's multicultural DNA, with exhibits and cultural events throughout. This feast for art lovers features paintings, sculptures, installations, drawings, photographs, and films of the highest quality, which are available throughout the city's best galleries and museums during that week. Check the website for ticket and event information.

Miami Beach Convention Center
1901 Convention Center Dr., Miami Beach
miamibeachconvention.com

EXPLORE THE EXOTIC
AT FAIRCHILD TROPICAL
BOTANIC GARDEN

Fairchild is the largest tropical botanic garden in the continental United States, with eighty-three acres of beautiful greenery, rare palms, trees, sunken gardens, and a spectacular 560-foot vine pergola. Take the tram tour first and see the most fantastic flora and fauna. Have your camera ready as you spot many of the in-house, world-renowned Dale Chihuly's glass sculptures. Explore the two-acre Simons rain forest, which showcases tropical plants from around the world, complete with waterfall and stream. Visit the conservatory and museum that are home to many rare tropical plants and stop by our laboratory and learning center.

Internationally recognized as a leader in both Florida and international conservation, Fairchild Tropical Botanic Gardens has field programs in more than twenty countries, and their education program reaches more than 100,000 schoolchildren each year. Its million-dollar orchid program with its mobile STEM lab truck decorated in green with painted orchids travels to schools to bring their state-of-the-art mobile botanic micropropagation.

10901 Old Cutler Rd., Miami
305-667-1651

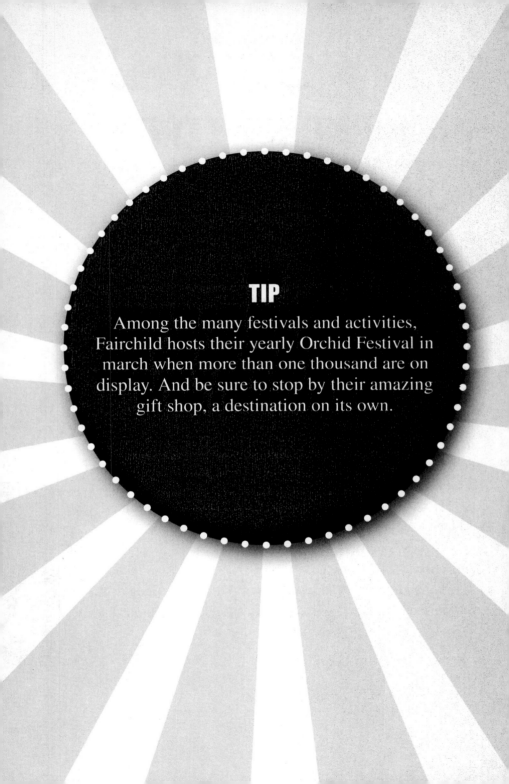

TIP

Among the many festivals and activities, Fairchild hosts their yearly Orchid Festival in march when more than one thousand are on display. And be sure to stop by their amazing gift shop, a destination on its own.

DO A CONGA LINE
SECOND SATURDAY IN MARCH

This is very large internationally renowned block party stretches for twenty blocks, and the music never stops. As a matter of fact, it gets louder and better whether you walk east or west and visit the more than a dozen stages filled with the best Latin musicians, bands, and street performers. You never know who might be there, as Calle Ocho has been the platform for some of the best Hispanic musicians today.

Calle Ocho festivities start in February with "Carnaval Miami" and the pageant and selection of "Miss Carnaval." Domino tournaments are held in Domino Park, and you can also find golf tournaments and festivities that run through the second Saturday in March with the world-famous Calle Ocho Festival, where more than a million spectators gather in this colorful extravaganza to celebrate Miami's Latin culture, food, and music. This was the stage for The Guinness World Records' "world's largest conga line," with 119,986 people dancing to the beat of Gloria Estefan.

So come and dance to the beat of salsa, merengue, and bachata, and relish in the baladas and boleros. Everyone dances in the streets that day, and even the rain gods join in and allow nothing in the sky but sunshine. Be a witness to the city's true multicultural character and lose yourself in the fun.

SW 8th St. (Calle Ocho) between 12th and 27th Aves.

TAKE A WALK
THROUGH WYNWOOD WALLS

Wynwood is not just artsy. Wynwood is art itself, like an outdoor museum of street and pop art showcasing large-scale murals by local and world-renowned street artists on every corner. As one of the city's most happening districts, it hosted its first street art exhibit in 2009 and has stolen the young hip crowd. Enter through the doors to check out Wynwood Walls, which is one of the most Instagrammed locations in the nation. Visitors flock to the funky streets on the second Saturday of every month and enjoy eating at the amazing restaurants and food trucks. One of the best ways to walk off the calories? Take the art murals bike tour or walk through the more than seventy art galleries and eclectic warehouses transformed into restaurants and shops just south of Miami's famed Design District.

NW 2nd Ave. between 23rd St. and 30th St., Miami

EXPERIENCE THE BEST OF CLASSICAL GUITAR
BROUGHT BY FLORIDA GUITAR FOUNDATION

Fighting for the number two spot of USA's cultural scene, Miami is bringing world-class performers who rival Carnegie Hall and Vienna's Konzerthaus.

Florida Guitar Foundation, a gem in our community, incites our young and vibrant cultural scene to raise the profile of classical guitar in Miami to a global level. Lining up the world's best classical guitarists for their concert season, you can now enjoy the much talked about revival of classical guitar in America and the diversities of its genre.

Concert Season: September–April at University of Miami's Frost School of Music.

Are you a guitar player? Come and participate in their monthly open mic. All ages, and levels of any guitar genre can participate, or check out their community guitar ensemble.

305-912-8343
floridaguitar.org

TIP

Miami will host the GFA (Guitar Foundation of America), the largest classical guitar convention and competition in the nation in conjunction with UM Frost School of Music and Florida Guitar Foundation. Check their website for dates.

BE DAZZLED
AT THE PHILLIP AND PATRICIA FROST MUSEUM OF SCIENCE

Before we talk about this cool museum, we will ask you to go right to level 4, Aquarium: the Vista, and just look out. Wow, what a view! You'll see Museum Park, downtown Miami, the Bay, and the PAMM right next door. This is just such a spectacular view that before you take anything else here, we want you to take in Miami. Now, turn around and learn about Miami at the Frost Museum. On level 4, learn about different marine life that call Miami home as well as the Everglades. Learn about the River of Grass and see an alligator up close! Children will love the opportunity to dip their hands into the Florida Bay exhibit and actually touch a sting ray! They'll get to see, touch, explore, and learn much more as you tour the Frost. This special space was a gift to Miami and now to you.

A dazzling $305 million world-class science museum with extensive exhibitions and a cutting-edge planetarium. The buildings' leading-edge sustainability initiatives are geared toward our future as a better planet. Witness twenty-first-century inventions in progress when you visit the inventors in the Residence Lab every day from 11:00 a.m. to 3:00 p.m. You can find everything science related in the

250,000-square-foor building complex consisting of the Aquarium, the Frost Planetarium, and the north and west wings. Don't miss the wildlife center and the weather and technology exhibits.

Located in Museum Park next to PAMM (Pérez Art Museum Miami)
1101 Biscayne Blvd., Miami
305-434-9600
frostscience.org

TIP
Don't leave without visiting level 2: the Deep. Make your way to the thirty-one-foot oculus lens and the bottom of the Aquarium, and look up at hammerhead sharks, tuna, and more swimming overhead. We suggest even lying on the floor to take it all in!

FIND GALLERY NIGHTS THROUGHOUT MIAMI

For art lovers, this is one of the best things this town has to offer. Every weekend enjoy free nights of art, sculptures, photography, and jewelry made by local artists. Galleries offer wine and vittles, but food trucks and music are also available to remind you that you are in Miami.

Wynwood Art Walk—The second Saturday of every month. Wynwood has stolen the art scene. This is the biggest of all and a favorite of the young art crowd. Insane fun, food trucks, and DJs. Don't miss it! Art enthusiasts and foodies find it all—culture, food, and a vibrant crowd. It's in the famous Art District of Miami.

Wynwood and Design District. You can do it all in one night.

Just north of downtown
Wynwood Art Walk—NW 2nd Ave. between 23rd and 30th Sts.

Design District Art Walk—The second Saturday of the month. It's a few blocks north of Wynwood, though a bit more conservative. You can do both in the same night.

Just North of Wynwood: NE 38th, 39th, and 40th Sts. between
N. Miami Ave. and NE 2nd Ave., miamidesigndistrict.com

Coral Gables Gallery Night—The City of Coral Gables pioneered gallery nights more than two decades ago. The first Friday of every month. It offers more classical and representational art. Surrounded by great restaurants and live music.

Ponce de Leon Blvd. in Coral Gables and surrounding streets.
Centered around Ponce Circle Park.

Viernes Culturales in Little Havana—The smallest of all the art events the last Friday ("Viernes" is Spanish for Friday) of the month. Cuban culture, nostalgia, and a love for America brought to life by local artists. Lots of Cuban food accompanied by music, dancing, and street performers a la Calle Ocho.

SW 8th Street (Calle Ocho) between SW 12th Ave. and SW 18th Ave.

MOCA Jazz Night (Museum of Contemporary Art)—On the last Friday of each month from 7:00 p.m. to 10:00 p.m. Art and vintage furniture with live jazz on the museum's front patio at 8:00 p.m.

Location: 770 NE 125th St.
305-893-6211 or visit mocanomi.org

Lincoln Road/South Beach—The first Saturday of the month. So much to do in Lincoln Road that you might forget why you are there. A favorite for those who do not want to leave the beach.

Location: Lincoln Road Open Mall

SEE VIBRANT COLORS
OF THE LEAH ARTS DISTRICT

Locals will tell you it's the least likely place they'd think to see new and emerging artists planting their painting roots, but Hialeah is certainly setting itself up for success in the art world. The City of Hialeah is saturated in the Cuban culture and proudly so. Don't get lost in Hialeah if you don't speak Spanish because most of the community are Spanish speakers. Hialeah continues to evolve and surprise many as it did with this space. Dubbed the Leah Arts District, a once gray, dreary, unwelcoming maze of factory walls now bursts with colors represented on the walls here. Not far from the famed Wynwood Walls, the Leah Arts District offers affordable living and creative spaces for these artists. You're also likely to find cafecito just around the corner!

1450 East 11th Ave., Hialeah
Leahartsdistrict.org
@leahartsdistrict

LET THE ROMANTIC IN YOU TAKE FLIGHT
AT MIAMI CITY BALLET

Russian-born choreographer George Balanchine is credited with creating contemporary American ballet. True to his choreography, Miami City Ballet has been hailed by *The New York Times* as "an exceptional troupe in Balanchine standards," and it ranks in the top ten ballet companies of the nation.

The Balanchine repertoire of more than four hundred dance choreographies is brought to life every year at the Arsht Center's Ziff Ballet Opera House, where people leap to their feet after each performance. Enjoy their breathtaking performances and marvelous choreographic craftsmanship when you are in town and let the romantic in you take flight to new heights.

Ziff Ballet Opera House
Adrienne Arsht Center for the Performing Arts
1300 Biscayne Blvd., Miami
305-946-6722
arshtcenter.org

PLAY, LEARN, IMAGINE AND CREATE
AT THE MIAMI CHILDREN'S MUSEUM

You might notice when you walk into the Miami Children's Museum that you have to bend down a bit to read all the facts to be learned that are posted on the museum's walls. That's when you realize that the Miami Children's Museum is created just for children. This is their world! It's the ultimate adventure land, where your child can dive into a creative and immersive world of art and music, science and technology! Children will learn with every hands-on activity—all with big smiles on their faces! Roxy's boys (one of this book's authors) are huge fans of the "South Florida and Me" gallery, where they can have fun "fishing," but children can enjoy the rotating exhibits, music, technology, and even special events during holidays that are perfectly planned just for your little ones.

Not to mention, Mom and Dad, this is an indoor, air-conditioned escape for the entire family! It gets really hot here in Miami, especially during the summer, which also brings rain most afternoons, so this is a great option to let your children run free while having educational fun!

980 MacArthur Causeway, Miami
305-373-5437
@miamichildrensmuseum

TIP

Every second Saturday of the month is Sensory Friendly Saturdays, offering awesome experiences for children with autism spectrum disorder, sensory processing disorder, and global developmental delays.

MEET OTHER BIBLIOPHILES
AT THE MIAMI BOOK FAIR

Every year hundreds of thousands of people come from all over the country to celebrate books, reading, and the experience of diving into a story, a recipe, or a child's picture book. The Miami Book Fair is the nation's premier literary festival, which since its inaugural year in 1984 has grown to welcome more than 450 authors to read and discuss their work. As with all things Miami, the Miami Book Fair is more than a festival. It is an event that is celebrated as a literary party over the course of eight days in mid-November. There are events at night, moderated panel discussions with authors throughout the week, and the highly anticipated Street Fair kicks off with thousands of schoolchildren from across South Florida on Friday.

The Children's Alley is full of interactive activities for children of all ages, which include reading and writing, storytelling, theater, music, art, and a section just for teens. Don't miss the Kitchen section, where you will find authors demonstrating recipes from their cookbooks for you to taste.

The Center for Literature and Theater at MDC
401 NE 2nd Ave., Miami
miamibookfair.com

TAKE IN SPECTACULAR VIEWS
AT PÉREZ ART MUSEUM MIAMI

Aesthetically breathtaking and designed by award-winning Swiss architects, the Pérez Art Museum of Miami (PAMM) is the centerpiece of Miami's innovative cultural life. Miami's rich culture and ethnicity are reflected in its ambience.

The first thing you see is dangling fish boats by the entrance designed by British artist Hew Locke. Also yachts and makeshift rafts to remind us of those who come by sea seeking refuge here and depicting Miami's maritime culture. Biscay Bay's turquoise waters in the backdrop set the stage for this provocative museum, with stairs that double as a theater. The terrace outside is spectacular, and you can relax in one of the Adirondack chairs while watching the cruise liners come and go.

Some people come back just to visit Verde, their amazing restaurant with such dishes as chicory and pear salad, butternut squash and fig pizza, shrimp tacos al pastor, and bucatini pasta. Guests will be dazzled, and additional tables, wooden booths, and banquettes have been added to the terrace for you to enjoy the view.

1103 Biscayne Blvd., Miami
305-375-8282
pamm.org

DISCOVER A CASTLE IN MIAMI
AT VIZCAYA MUSEUM AND GARDENS

California has Hearst Castle, but Miami has its counterpart right in the middle of the city and busy US1, and it's a treasured jewel: the Palace of Vizcaya, built more than a hundred years ago. Take a stroll through its Italian Renaissance gardens inspired by the Veneto region. Discover the beauty of its carved mantles, gilded panels, and fresco ceilings imported directly from Tuscany and France, and leave the noise behind to experience this sanctuary of silence and green. This reproduction of an eighteenth-century Mediterranean Italian villa—now museum—was designed for Miami's subtropical climate. The Palace's main house has an open courtyard to view the warm, clear nights of the city.

If you want to experience a magical night, stroll the gardens by moonlight and enjoy live music in the courtyards. Sip on some wine and feel as royalty did many years ago.

The Palace hosts several Renaissance-themed events throughout the year.

vizcaya.org/home.asp

GET ON BOARD
AT THE MIAMI INTERNATIONAL BOAT SHOW

Showcasing our sunny city and fun lifestyle, the Miami International Boat Show comes to town every year during the second week in February.

After thirty years, the show has moved from Miami Beach to the Miami Marine Stadium in Virginia Key. Now you can come to the show by land or sea! With more transportation options, you can catch a free water taxi at Bayfront Park, the American Airlines Arena, or the complimentary shuttle buses. They run all day.

See every boat manufactured under one roof. From a small kayak to the largest of yachts, this is boater's heaven. Take one of their training or boat classes and don't miss the opportunity to ask the experts on hand any questions you need answered to learn all you want about boating.

Miami Marine Stadium
Virginia Key

CELEBRATE THE COLORS OF THE COMMUNITY
AT MIAMI BEACH GAY PRIDE

All the colors of the rainbow come together in Miami Beach for a grand celebration of the unique spirit, culture, diversity, and equality of the LGBTQ community with PRIDE. Miami Beach Gay Pride goes beyond a fabulous parade. There's a slew of festivities culminating in a grand PRIDE parade along historic Ocean Drive. The LGBTQ community and allies come together from all over the world freely, safely, and equally to celebrate individuality, peace, and love among one another. Though Miami Beach celebrates equality every day of the year, this free event is the ultimate celebration of expressionism and individualism supported in love and respect by so many who come from all over the world to be a part of PRIDE in Miami Beach.

Events take place all across Miami; check their website for specific locations.

Miami Beach Gay Pride
miamibeachgaypride.com
@miamibeachgaypride

TAKE IN THE ART AL FRESCO
AT COCONUT GROVE ARTS FESTIVAL

Ranked among the top five in America's Best Art Fairs 2013, this festival showcases more than 350 internationally renowned artists, culinary demonstrations, live music, and dance performances. More than one thousand applicants from all over the world compete to earn a spot at this prestigious event. Pick up great art pieces that range from fifteen dollars to tens of thousands for original paintings in a laid-back display.

CEO and president Monty Trainer (owner of Monty's Raw Bar) is the force behind this "art on the water" event that is now in its fifty-sixth year and has added culinary demonstrations. "Food is a form of art," he says. Be sure to mark this as one of your destinations.

South Bayshore Dr., Coconut Grove

TIP
Attend during the President's Day Holiday Weekend (third Monday in February). Around fifteen dollars per person.

ROLL OUT THE RED CARPET
AT THE MIAMI INTERNATIONAL FILM FESTIVAL

The best of the world's cinema has passed through the screens of the Miami Film Festival. Also known by its other official name, Miami International Film Festival, this ten-day showcase brings a multitude of independent and international films from all corners of the globe to make their world premiere during this highly anticipated event in the month of March. The Miami International Film Festival is a true testimony to the city's cultural prominence and serves as a platform for filmmakers, critics, and the film industry in general with more than eighty thousand attendees from more than sixty countries around the globe, including some of the most well-known names in cinema both on the screen and behind it—from Anne Hathaway and Christopher Plummer to filmmakers Pedro Almodódvar and Alfonso Cuarón. Premiere night and the most anticipated world premieres are held at the historic Gusman Cultural Center, with movie screenings held in various theaters throughout Miami.

Check the website for schedules and tickets.

miamifilmfestival.com

SAMPLE THE BEST OF THE BEST
AT THE SOUTH BEACH WINE AND FOOD FESTIVAL

Are you a fan of food? Are you a fan of celebrity chefs? Do you like making a difference in the lives of students aspiring to be the next celebrity chefs? We're certainly hoping you answered YES because the Food Network and Cooking Channel South Beach Food and Wine Festival needs to be on your Miami bucket list. This festival goes beyond any other food festival you've ever attended. Let's start with the fact that you're having the best bites served on the sands of South Beach. The star talent from the Food Network descends on South Florida—chefs Bobby Flay, Giada De Laurentiis, Geoffrey Zakarian, Scott Conant, Alex Guarnaschelli, Masaharu Morimoto, and so many more! They're not out of reach either. You can see them, speak with them, and eat food prepared by them and their team! There are so many events, from seminars to sit-downs to tastings of foods from all parts of the country and the world. What makes all this that much sweeter is that proceeds benefit the Florida International University's Chaplin School of Hospitality and Tourism Management, which to date has raised more than $28 million. Raise a glass to that!

sobewff.com
@sobewffest

TIP

There are several events all over Miami and beyond. Check their website for more and tickets.

SHOPPING AND FASHION

CHECK OFF YOUR "TO DO" LIST
AT LINCOLN ROAD MALL

So, what do you need? What do you hope to find? What's your craving? Come to Lincoln Road Mall and you'll likely check all those boxes on that "to do" list here! This mile-long stretch of pedestrian-friendly space is lined with brand-name stores, exclusive boutiques, quaint cafes, high-end restaurants, and entertainment too. Find what you need or what you never knew you needed, and then sit at one of the outdoor cafes for lunch, brunch, ice cream, coffee, or all of the above to celebrate your new purchase. As the sun starts to set, have a cocktail, sit back and people watch. Open your eyes and your ears to languages from all around the world. Lincoln Road Mall is a must-stop destination for first-time visitors to Miami and returning guests. Watch a movie at Regal Cinemas or walk over one block to the New World Center, where free movies are projected on a 7,000-square-foot wall for Miami Beach SoundScape! Bring a blanket and pack a snack to catch a movie under the Miami moon.

Lincoln Rd., Miami Beach
@LincolnRoadMall

TIP
Swing by on Sundays for fresh vegetables, fruit, snacks, and more at its farmers market.

BE TRANSPORTED TO SPAIN WITHOUT LEAVING MIAMI
AT ESPAÑOLA WAY

Tucked away from the hustle and bustle of Miami Beach is an escape into two charming blocks of a historic Spanish Village. During the day, the Mediterranean stucco sticks out as unique. At night, the twinkling cafe lights strung from building to building illuminate the promenade and call to you to come for a cocktail, a cafe, shopping, dinner, or dancing. You're about three blocks away from famed Lincoln Road Mall, but this experience is different. It's romantic. Scope out art galleries, unique products, and collectibles. Have some Spanish tapas, or take a taste of French or Italian food, which also plays to the surroundings.

Between Washington Ave. and Pennsylvania Ave.
and 14th St. and 15th St., Miami Beach
305-672-127
@MiamiandBeaches

PLAN A DAY
AT BRICKELL CITY CENTRE

This is a reboot we never knew we needed. Brickell City Centre has not only changed Miami's skyline, but it's also reinvigorated the city, the locals, and has given visitors another must-stop destination to add to their Miami bucket list. Brickell City Centre sounds grand, and it is an incredibly awesome innovative and creative space that has quickly become one of Miami's bragging points. It's a place to shop, eat, sit, sip, stay, and live.

You're greeted by three levels of shopping, dining, and entertainment—clean and modern lines with lush landscaping that subtly brings the outdoors in. Anchored by Saks Fifth Avenue, you'll see many luxury retail stores, name brands, high-end labels, and international brands. The dining experience stands out on its own, with locals coming here just to eat! You should too! Head to the third and fourth floors to explore the sweet and savory, from steak to sushi! La Centrale is an Italian food hall offering fourteen different Italian options for you to enjoy.

Overhead walkways were built with you in mind, connecting BCC over three blocks of Downtown Miami. As you walk about discovering this beautiful space, look up. That's more than just awesome architecture. That's the Climate Ribbon. Beyond being just beautiful, it serves a purpose. It protects pedestrians, cafes, and store fronts from rain and the sun and naturally ventilates the space too. It is also a natural canal that collects rainwater, which is used for planting and irrigation. From the ground and especially from the sky, it's a symbol of sustainability.

701 S Miami Ave., Miami
786-475-4932
brickellcitycentre.com
@brickellcitycentre

TIP

Make your way to EAST Miami hotel, which is part of Brickell City Centre. Miami is the flagship city for EAST in the United States after Hong Kong and Beijing. It's a beautiful hotel, modern and luxurious with an award-winning bar called Sugar on the roof. The view is spectacular.

BE INSPIRED
BY INNOVATIVE AND HIGH-END
FASHION IN THE DESIGN DISTRICT

Fashion, art, décor, and design. The Miami Design District continues to evolve and explode as a must-stop destination for shopping and inspiration. The coveted streets of the Miami Design District are lined with high-end brand names: Fendi, Dior, Givenchy, Hermes, Christian Louboutin, and more. Add that luxurious fashion piece you've dreamed of or merely take it all in walking the District, and snap a selfie to social. Don't miss out on the innovative art pieces around as well, especially the *Fly's Eye Dome*, a variation of late architect and designer Buckminster Fuller's work, that sits center at Palm Court. It's become a landmark in photos that says "I'm in the Design District" and serves as the backdrop during the Miami Design District Performance Series, produced by 19-time Grammy Award winner (and just an awesome guy) Emilio Estefan outside of Estefan Kitchen.

3841 NE 2nd Ave., Miami
305-722-7100
@miamidesigndistrict

VISIT
SOUTH FLORIDA'S FIRST HIGH-END SHOPPING CENTER AT BALL HARBOUR SHOPS

As Miami continues to emerge as one of the most popular high-end fashion destinations in the country, we can look to where the high-end labels went to first—Bal Harbour Shops. This is an open-air mall where the rich and famous come to purchase the finer things, from fine china to luxury handbags and everything in between. If your budget won't allow you to swipe your credit card, just come and walk through the outdoor mall and make plans for lunch here—from sushi to Italian and a more classic American bistro menu. We're fans of heading up to the third floor at Neiman Marcus and taking a seat at Zodiac for a fresh salad or sandwich and the mouthwatering piping-hot popover served to start with a side of strawberry butter! There's a reason why Bal Harbour Shops has been a leader in luxury retail since 1965 as Florida's first high-fashion shopping center. It is still revered as a destination to shop high-end brands al fresco situated between the Intracoastal and the Ocean. By the way, when you valet or park your car, be sure to look around at all the cool, fancy cars parked around the garage, from Bentleys to Ferraris!

9700 Collins Ave., Bal Harbour
305-866-0311
balharbourshops.com

STROLL, SHOP, AND SIP
AT THE SHOPS IN THE GABLES

Locals love spending time in and around "The City Beautiful," Coral Gables. There are so many quaint shops and restaurants to check out around the Gables. You'll certainly get a taste of all that when you visit the Shops at Merrick Park. This is an open-air mall, with beautiful landscaping, water fountains, and so many options to eat outdoors under umbrellas in the shopping promenade's courtyard. The shopping is extensive. There's a lot to look at, and other shopping options are available beyond the high price tag. Whether you're shopping for the children, the home, or yourself, browse brand and luxury labels and options for a variety of budgets. This is also a beautiful space to visit during the holidays, with beautiful decorations throughout the shops celebrating all the seasons and holidays!

358 San Lorenzo Ave., Coral Gables
305-529-0200
@shopsatmerrickpark

SHOP FOR VINTAGE AND VINYL RECORDS,
CLASSIC TUNES
IN THE MOST CLASSIC WAY

It was hard for us to pick just one place to add to your bucket list to pick up music and pay homage to vinyl, so here are our top three picks:

Technique Records opened in 2018 with pros at the helm of your music buying experience. They have vinyls, tapes, and cult movies as they put it all up for grabs and are also known to have famous faces drop in for signings.

Museo Del Disco literally translates to museum of discs. I guess if you ask the younger generation, they would believe that vinyl and tapes belong in a museum, right? Wrong! This is a hidden gem and off the beaten path and known by locals (and now you) as a place to come to find what you're looking for. Don't be thrown off by the Spanish. You'll find all the classics here.

Sweat Records is an indie record shop in the most unassuming space offering classic on vinyl but also tea, vegan treats, and at times live music or stand-up comedians on their main stage.

Technique Records, 853 NE 79th St., Miami
Museo Del Disco, 1301 S.W. 70th Ave., Miami
Sweat Records, 5505 NE 2nd Ave., Miami, 786-639-9309
@sweatrecords

FALL IN LOVE WITH A STORY
AT BOOKS & BOOKS

In a world where so many of us are constantly looking down at devices, come here and look up. Disconnect from technology and reconnect with the world around you by jumping into the pages of a book. For generations, words have painted the pages and told a story in a book, but technology has hit the "delete" button in many cases for thumbing through the pages. These days most people just "swipe" and "tap." Technology is great, but it's nice to embrace the experience, and it's not gone. Come to Books & Books in Coral Gables and you can smell the wooden bookcases that hold so many adventures just wanting to be read! Mitchell Kaplan, founder of Books & Books, opened his first store in 1982 in the heart of Coral Gables, and today, across the street from the original location, a quaint neighborhood bookstore takes you back to basics, back to the magic and intimate moment of searching, finding, and falling in love with a story printed on pages of an actual book—just like the one in your hands right now!

Books & Books in Coral Gables
265 Aragon Ave., Coral Gables
booksandbooks.com
@booksandbooks

TIP

Several Books & Books are located all around South Florida, with some locations offering a cafe for you to enjoy while reading! Check out the website for details.

SUGGESTED
ITINERARIES

DATE NIGHT

SUN AND SURF

FUN WITH THE KIDS

OUTDOOR ADVENTURES

CULTURAL AFFAIRS

INDEX